LEARN AS YOU PLAY TROMBONE & EUPHONIUM

BASS CLEF EDITION

BY PETER WASTALL

Revised edition 1990

Learn As You Play is a series of instrumental tutors designed specifically to prepare pupils for the early grades of all the principal examination boards. The tutors are suitable for both individual and group instruction.

The course, which is divided into 24 units, places the maximum emphasis on the early development of musicianship. From the beginning it introduces the student to a wide range of music, including works by leading contemporary composers. Each unit contains the following teaching programme:

1
New material is presented in clear progressive steps

2
Short, concise exercises enable new skills to be quickly developed

3
Instrumental solos by distinguished composers stimulate and develop practice repertoire

4
Progressive technical studies gradually bring the student into contact with specific instrumental technique

5
Instrumental duets (alternate units) provide experience in ensemble playing. Keyboard accompaniments to the duets can be added in early units

Progress is measured at eight-unit intervals by the introduction of Concert Pieces which utilise all previously learned material

Piano accompaniments are available for these pieces in a separate accompaniment book. The Concert Pieces are works representative of examination requirements and in many instances are works which have been set in current or past syllabuses.

SERIES EDITOR
PETER WASTALL

Trombone assembly

To assemble the trombone, first ensure that the slide is in its closed position with the slide ring locked. Next fit the slide section into the bell section so that they form a 90° angle. The slide must be to the right of the bell with the water key at the bottom. Finally, lock the two sections together by tightening the locking ring attached to the bell section.

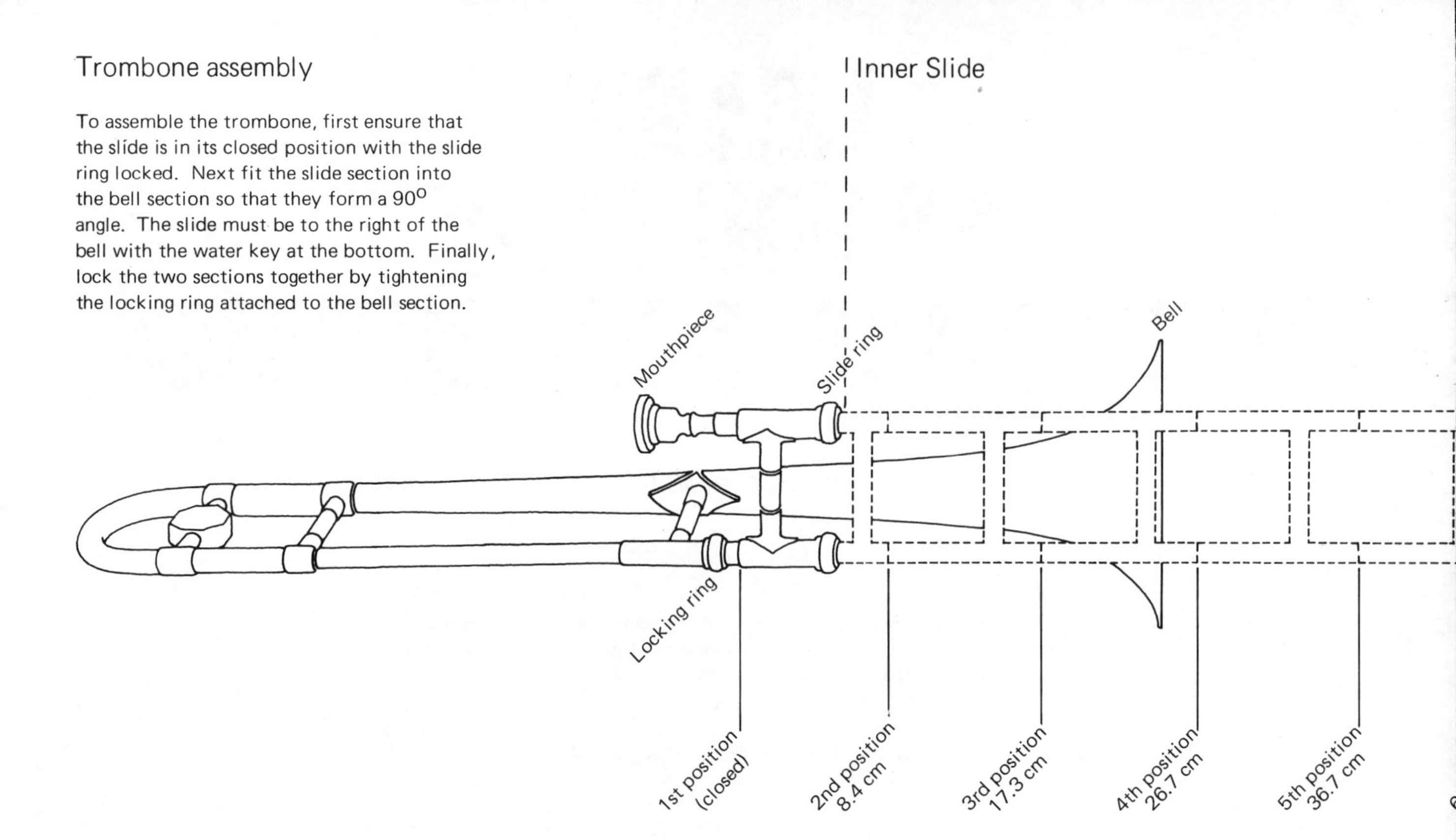

Trombone slide positions

The slide position measurements are approximate since small variations occur between different makes of instrument. For beginners, here is a useful guide:

3rd position: right hand index finger opposite the bell.

4th position: the end of the outer slide just past the bell.

Sound production

In keeping with other brass instruments, the trombone and euphonium have a range of notes that can be produced without moving the slide or depressing any valves. Usually a pupil's first notes are either B♭, F or low B♭. The main objective will be to play F. If the first notes are higher than F, relax the muscles at the lip centre. If the first notes are lower than F, firm the muscles around the aperture.

Points to remember

1. Hold the mouthpiece lightly against the lips with just enough pressure to stop air escaping.

2. Never allow the cheeks to balloon outwards.

3. Position the jaw so that both lips can vibrate freely.

4. Trombonists should check that the third and fourth position notes are in tune by listening and comparing them with the first position notes.

Trombone hand positions

Notice how the left hand supports the trombone, holding it evenly balanced so that the slide can move easily. The right hand controls the slide without creating excessive wrist movement.

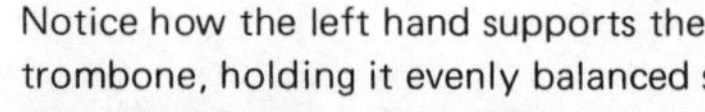

Mouthpiece placement

The mouthpiece is usually placed centrally on the lips, with two thirds of the top lip and one third of the bottom lip showing inside the mouthpiece when a visualiser is used.

Euphonium

The Euphonium is supported by the left hand enabling the right hand fingertips to be positioned over the valves.

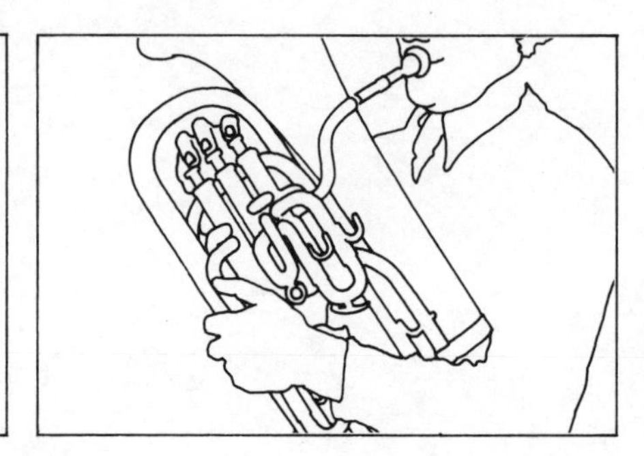

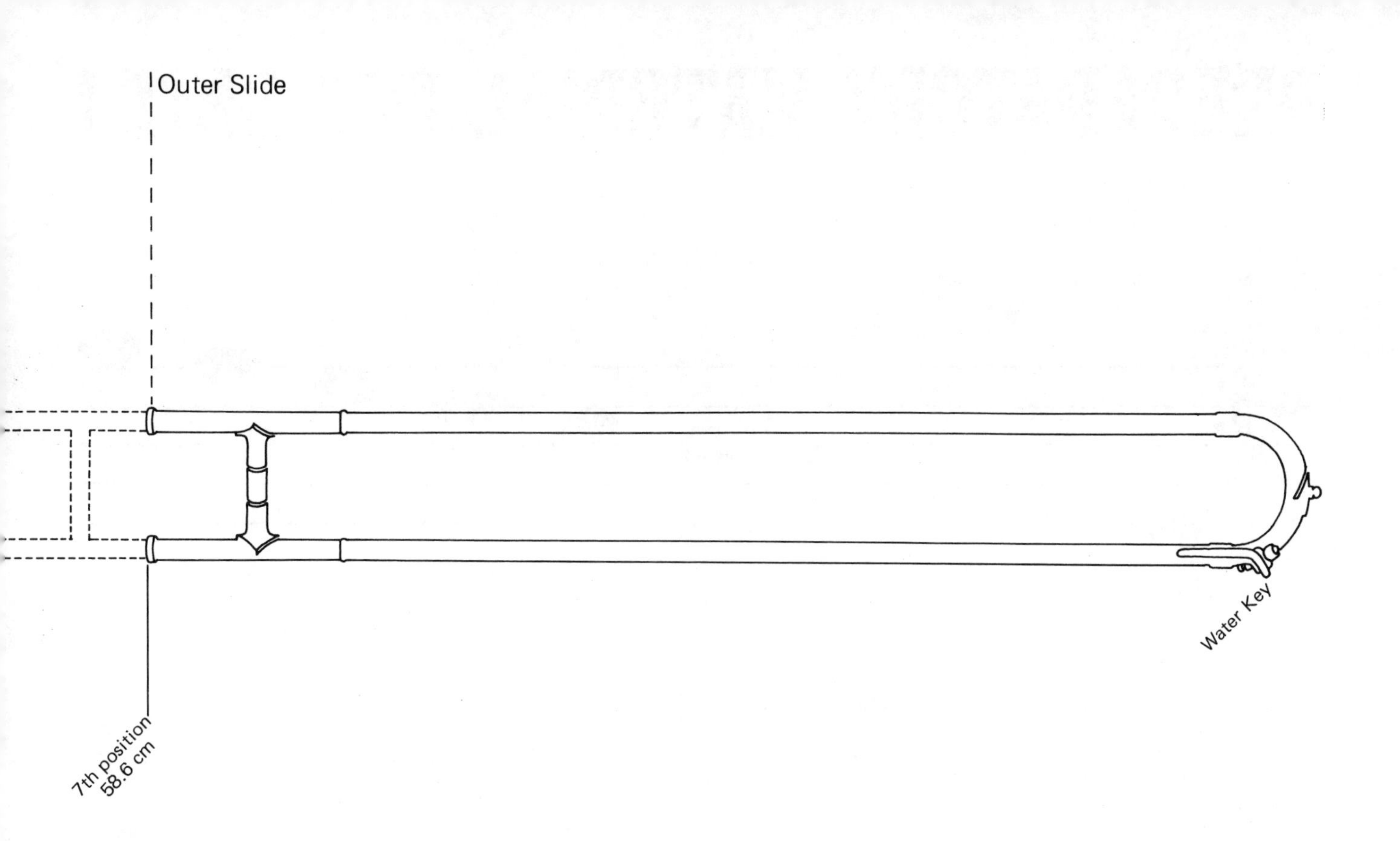

After experimenting with the first position notes, compare the sounds B♭, A♭, G, F and E♭.

Start each note with a tongue movement similar to that used when pronouncing the letter 'T'.

	B♭	A♭	G	F	E♭
Trombone slide position	1	3	4	1	3
Euphonium fingering	Open	1	1 2	Open	1

PREPARATORY MATERIAL FOR UNIT 1

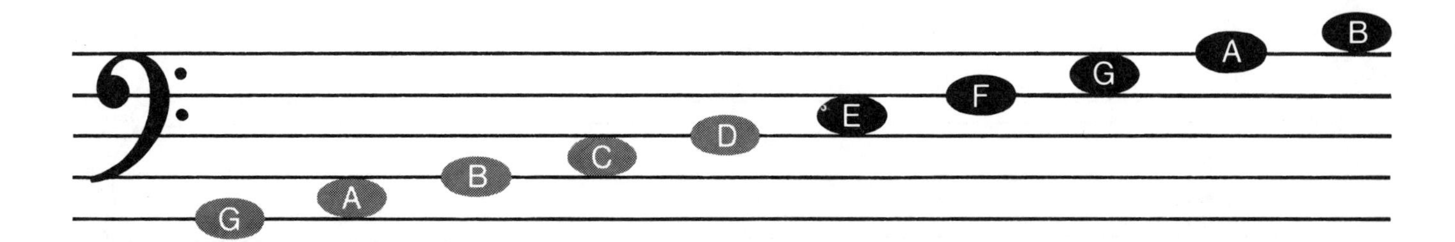

Notation

Printed notes are also named after the first seven letters of the alphabet. From the example it can be seen that they are placed on a staff (the name of the five lines), each line and each space counting as one letter name.

The Bass Clef

Since the same seven letter names are used for all instruments (i.e. those that produce high notes, as well as those that produce low notes) a clef sign is placed at the beginning of each staff to establish exact pitch; usually, trombone and euphonium music is written in the bass clef.

Note Lengths

The length of time a note is played is measured by the beat; the difference in length being shown by various types of note. The three types used in unit 1 are:

crotchet minim semibreve

Play the following crotchets trying to hold each for exactly the same amount of time.

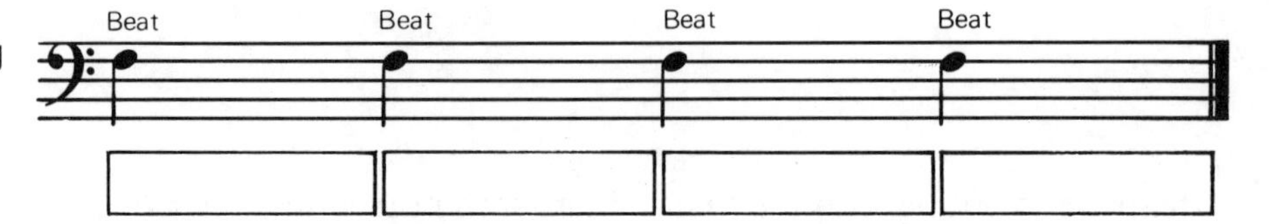

Now play the following minims, holding each note for the whole of beats one and two added together.

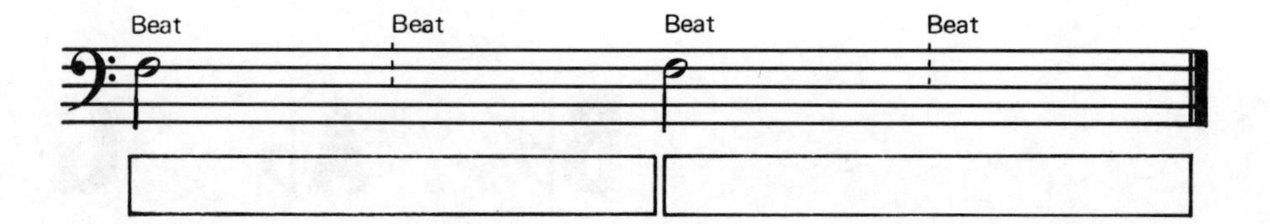

Now play a semibreve, trying to hold the note for exactly four beats.

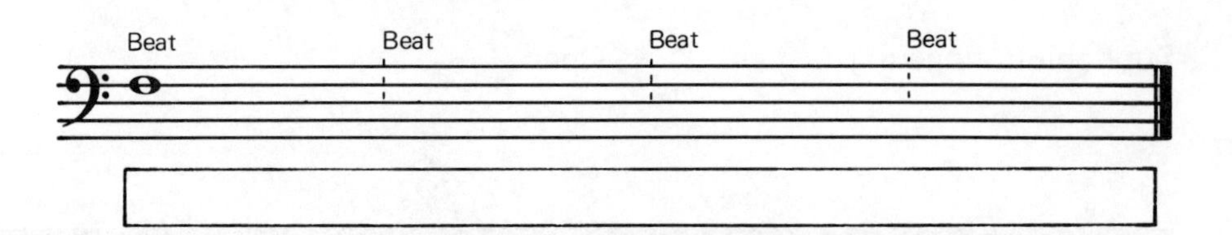

Bars and bar lines

Bar line | Double bar line

Beats usually group themselves into regular patterns of either two, three or four; to show these patterns, the music is divided by bar lines into bars.

A double bar line is used to separate differing sections of music within a single piece.

A thin/thick double bar indicates the end of a piece or exercise.

Time Signatures

A time-signature is placed at the beginning of each piece of music to show how many beats there are in a bar, and the type of note that equals one beat. It is printed in fractional form, the value of the crotchet being shown as a fraction of a semibreve.

$\frac{2}{4}$ showing 2 crotchet beats in each bar

$\frac{3}{4}$ showing 3 crotchet beats in each bar

$\frac{4}{4}$ showing 4 crotchet beats in each bar

UNIT 1

Flat Signs

Every note in music can be raised or lowered half a tone. The sign for lowering a note half a tone is the flat sign shown in the example. During units 1 and 2, flat signs will be used to show B♭, A♭ and E♭.

Notes and Slide positions (summarised from p. 2 - 5)

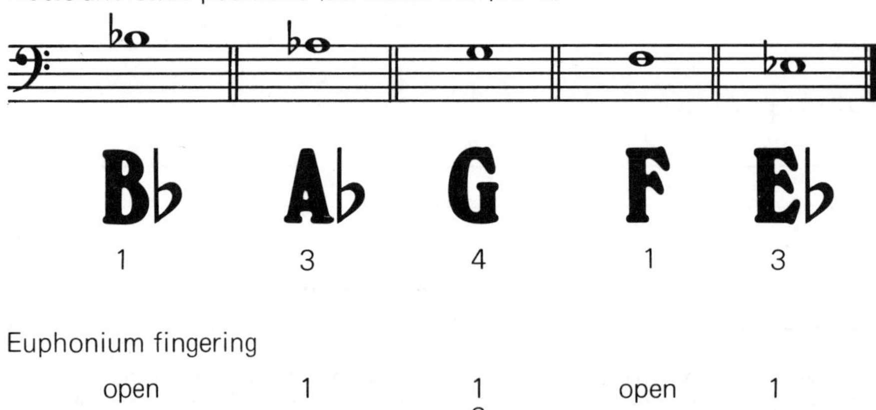

Exercise 1

Exercise 2

Exercise 3

Exercise 4

Exercise 5

Musicianship

When you practise the instrumental solos, notice how the notes form patterns almost as if they were words in a rhyme. In music these note patterns are called phrases; to help identify them, phrases in some early pieces have been marked with brackets. Breaths are normally taken at the ends of phrases; additional breaths can be taken, but these must be discreet so as not to disturb the natural flow of the phrase.

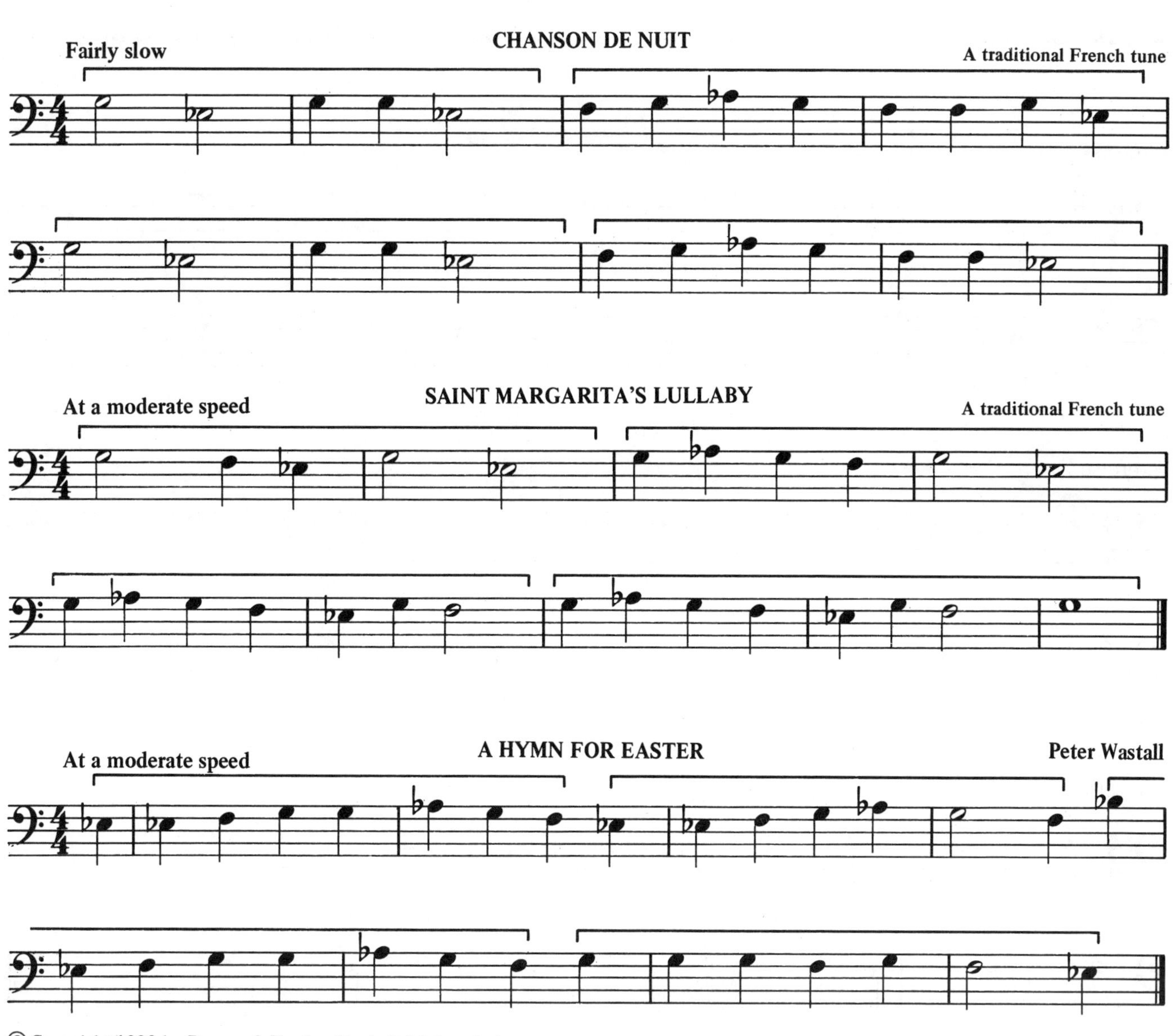

UNIT 2

The Pause sign

When a pause sign is placed over a note, the beat stops and the note is played for a period of time longer than its printed value. During the first section of this book the pause will be used mainly in the exercises, identifying individual notes that are to be sustained for as long as possible.

Rests

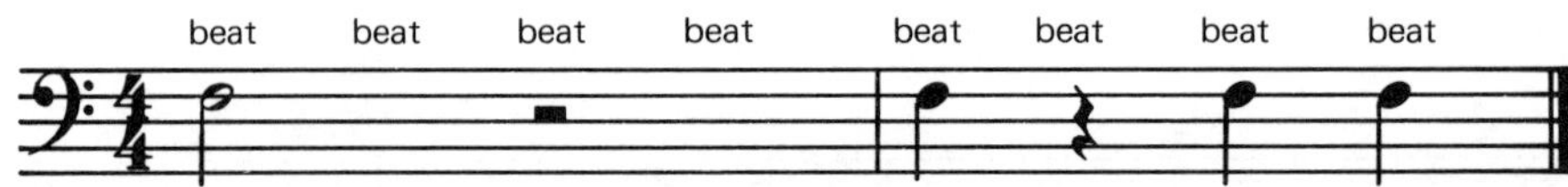

The length of time in which notes are not played is shown by various rests, each note having an equivalent rest. The example shows the minim rest (two beats of silence) and the crotchet rest (one beat of silence).

FFIGYSBREN

Tone development

One of the best ways to develop a full tone is to play individual long notes. In the exercise that follows, listen closely to the sound and check these vital points.

1. Diaphragm giving a light support to the air stream.
2. Instrument held in such a position that both lips can vibrate freely.
3. Facial muscles firm, but not gripping.

LET'S BEGUINE

(A duet for pupil and teacher)

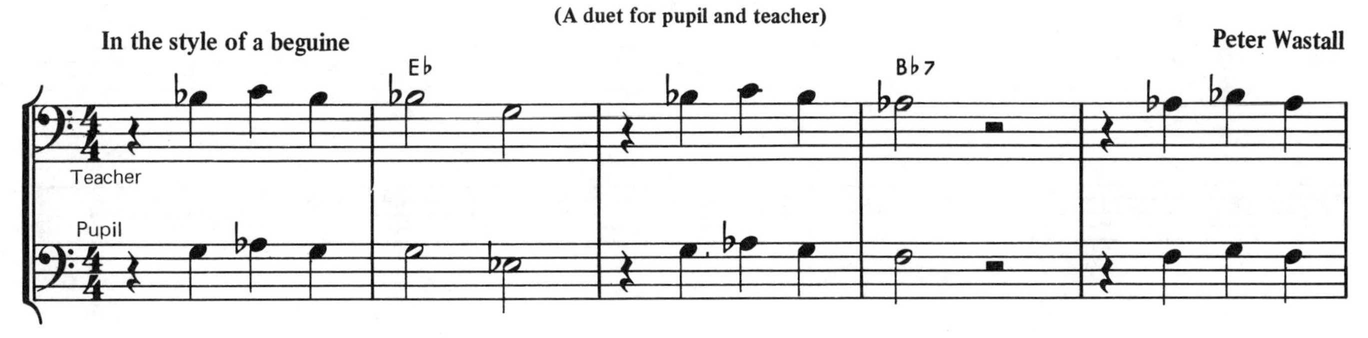

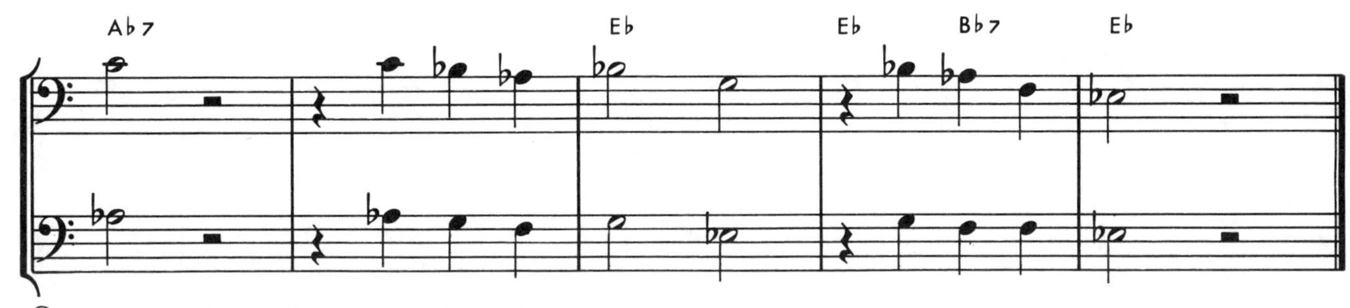

UNIT 3

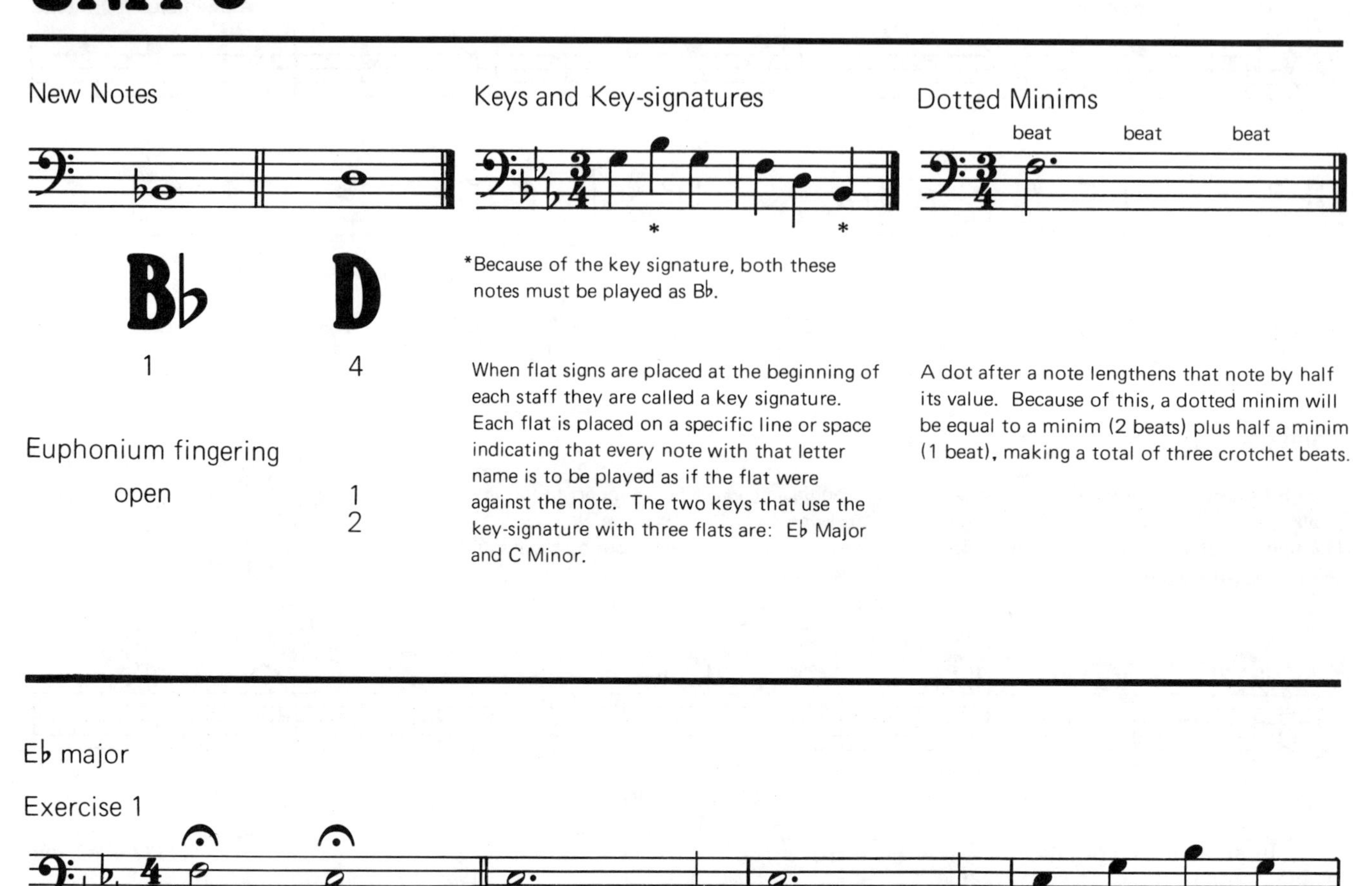

New Notes

B♭ — 1

D — 4

Euphonium fingering

	B♭	D
	open	1 2

Keys and Key-signatures

*Because of the key signature, both these notes must be played as B♭.

When flat signs are placed at the beginning of each staff they are called a key signature. Each flat is placed on a specific line or space indicating that every note with that letter name is to be played as if the flat were against the note. The two keys that use the key-signature with three flats are: E♭ Major and C Minor.

Dotted Minims

A dot after a note lengthens that note by half its value. Because of this, a dotted minim will be equal to a minim (2 beats) plus half a minim (1 beat), making a total of three crotchet beats.

E♭ major

Exercise 1

Exercise 2

Exercise 3

Exercise 4

Musicianship

The ability to remember melodic phrases plays an important part in the development of musicianship. To help develop a melodic memory, try each week to memorise one of the shorter instrumental solos.

The grade 1 aural tests issued by the Associated Board of the Royal Schools of Music will help memory development and should be incorporated into the lesson at this stage.

UNIT 4

Semibreve Rests

A semibreve rest is used to show any complete bar of rest, regardless of the number of beats in the bar. When it occurs you must examine the time-signature to find the number of beats to be counted. Compare the three examples.

Ties

A tie is a curved line placed over or under two notes of the same pitch. The tie joins the notes together making one continuous note. In order to produce one continuous note the second note must not be tongued.

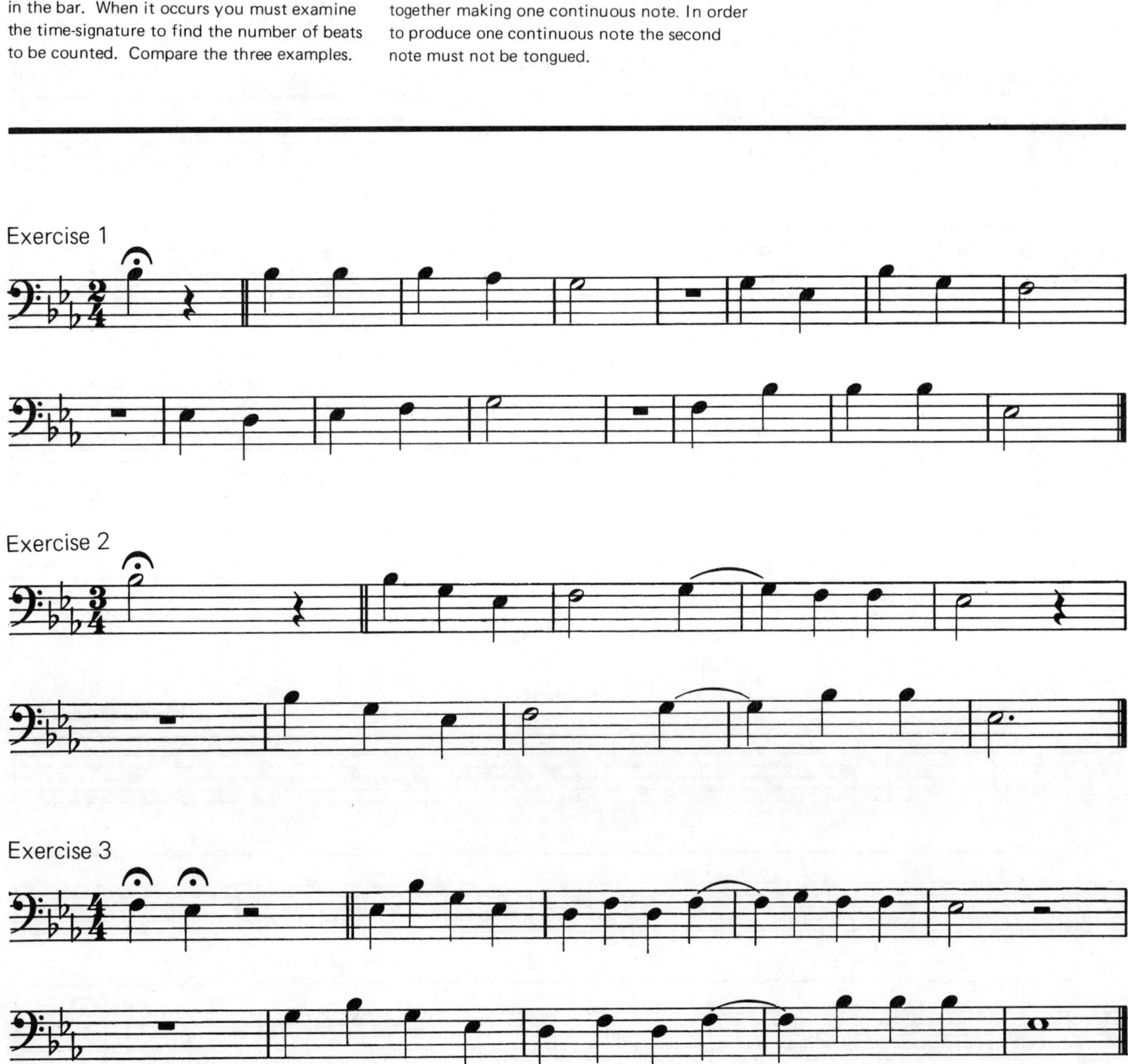

MARCH

"If all the world were paper"

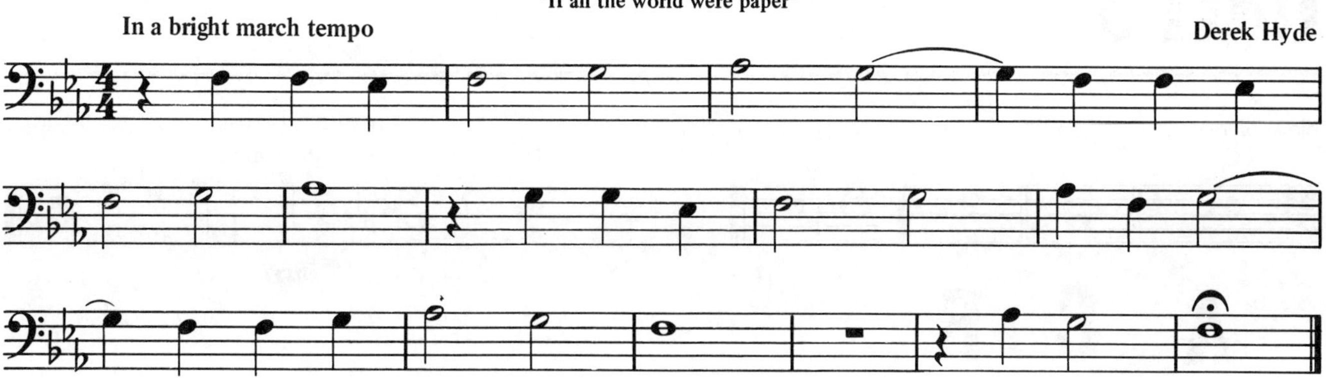

Tone development

1. Use exercise (a) for comparing the embouchure formation for playing open notes B♭-F-B♭.
2. Play the first note with a relatively strong air pressure, keeping the diaphragm moderately firm.
3. During the exercise, progressively lower the diaphragm and tongue levels by using the syllables 'TOO-TA-TAAH'.
4. Encourage the lips to vibrate freely, but keep the corners of the mouth in their correct position at all times.
5. Repeat the drill for each exercise.

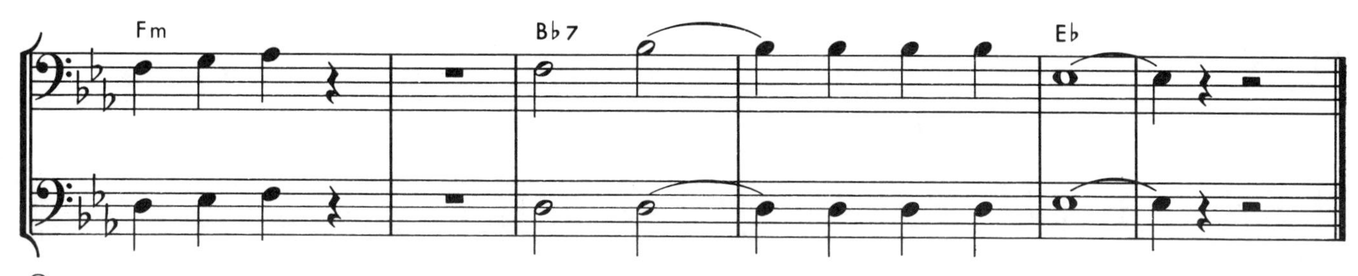

UNIT 5

New Notes

A **C** **F**

2 6 6

Euphonium fingering

2 $\frac{1}{3}$ or 4 *

A New Key-signature

In flat keys, the name of the major key can be found by counting four letter names down from the last flat. The example shows a key signature with two flats. Since the last flat is E♭ the name of the major key must be B♭ Major.

*Euphonium players should continue to use the open fingering unless otherwise stated.

Italian Terms

Andante

mp

Italian terms describe how fast a piece is to be played and how loud or soft the music should sound. The terms which describe how loud or soft the music should sound are usually abbreviated. A table of the abbreviations is printed in Unit 12 where this aspect of technique is developed. A list of Italian terms is printed at the end of the book.

B♭ Major

Exercise 1

Exercise 2

Exercise 3

mf

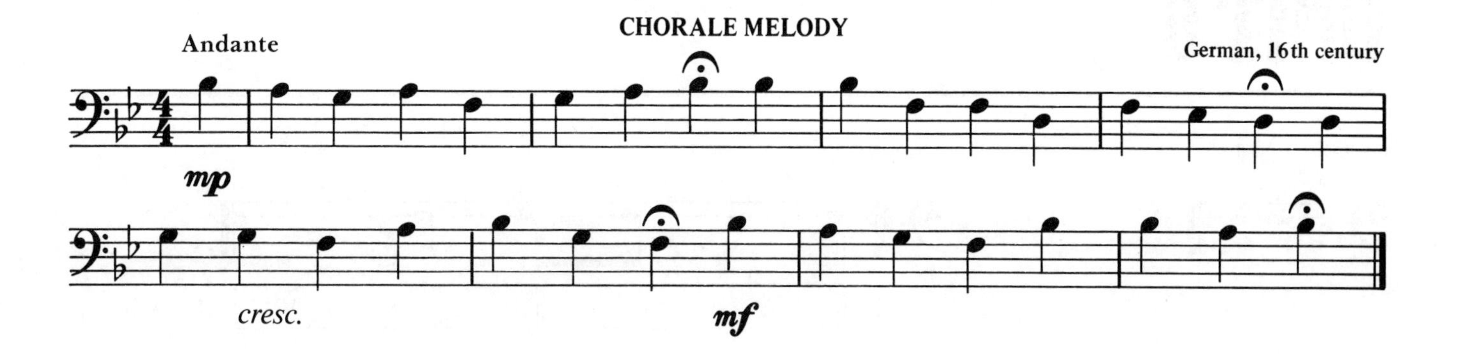

Trombone technique

1. Notice that F can be played in sixth position.
2. Use the first bar of each exercise to help tune the sixth position.
3. Keep the slide position still when changing to the C.
4. Listen carefully to the tuning of the pause notes. Each must be identical in pitch to the C already established.

UNIT 6

Staccato Marks

When a dot is placed over or under a note it indicates that the note is to sound detached. To achieve this, the note is played shorter than its printed value, often producing a clipped effect, rather like saying the word TAP.

Quavers

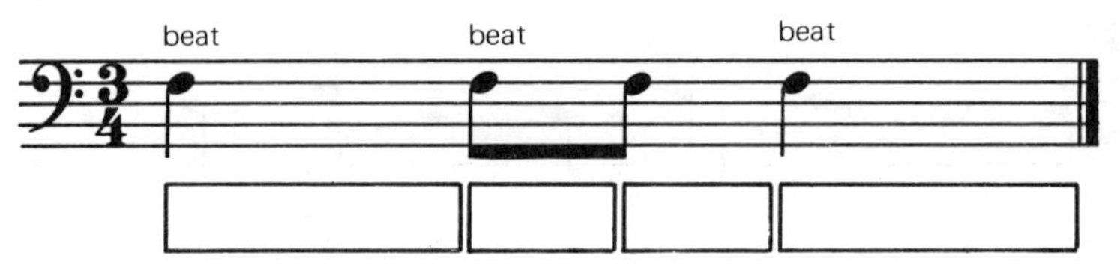

The value of a quaver is half a crotchet: it is printed with a tail on the end of its stem. For ease of reading, groups of quavers usually have their tails joined together.

Exercise 1

Exercise 2

Exercise 3

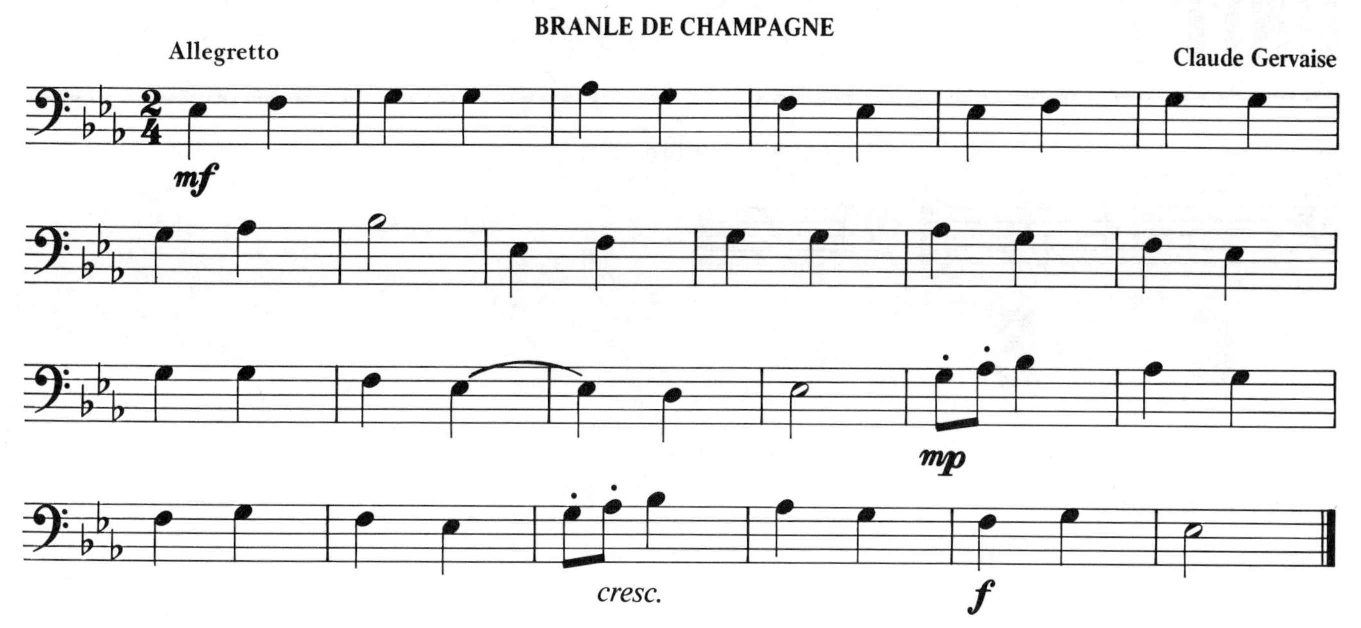

Aids to music reading

When you play quavers read them like a two-syllable word. For example, when you read the word 'Doctor', you don't read 'Doc' then 'tor', you read 'Doctor'. This 'block' reading skill should be developed at the earliest possible stage of music reading. To help this development, each time quavers occur, make a conscious effort to read both notes at the same time.

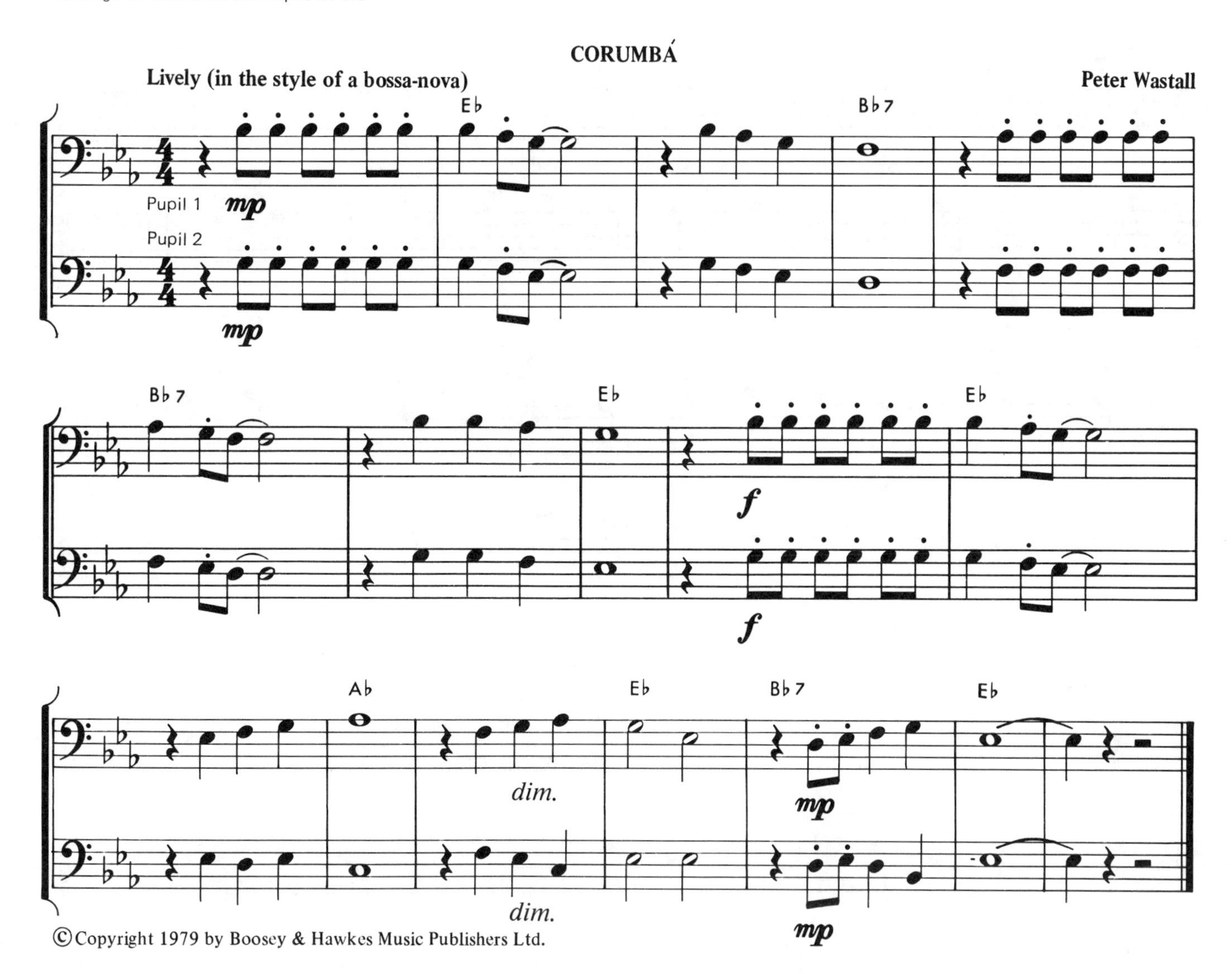

UNIT 7

New Notes

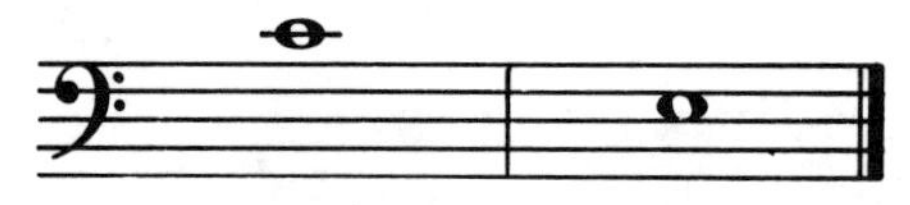

C   E

3   2

Euphonium fingering

1   2

A New Key-signature

The two keys that use the key-signature with one flat are F Major and D Minor. The music in this unit illustrates F Major.

F Major

Exercise 1

Exercise 2

Exercise 3

Tone development

1. Use this set of exercises to develop maximum vibration at the lip centre.
2. Check that the facial muscles are properly formed at all times, particularly the corners of the mouth outside the mouthpiece.
3. As you descend, enlarge the mouth cavity by slightly opening the gap between the teeth.

UNIT 8

New Notes | Repeat Signs | Slurs

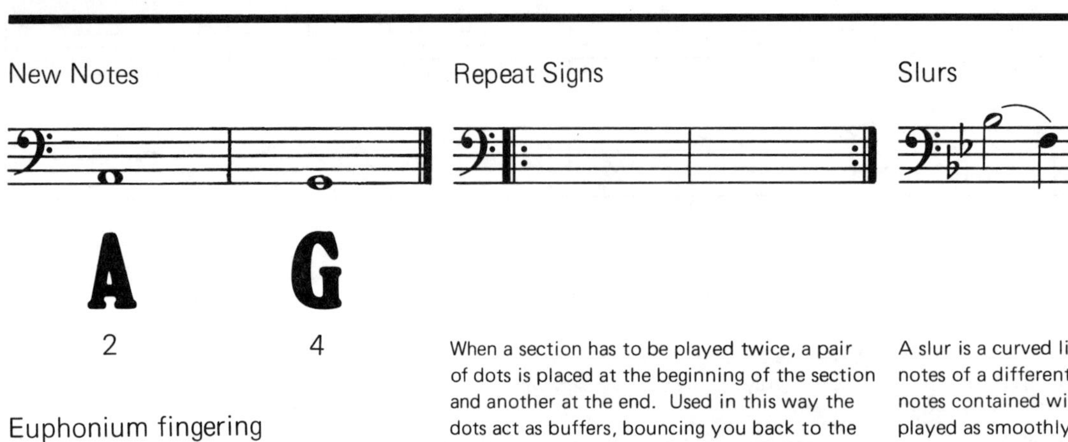

A **G**

2 4

Euphonium fingering

2 1
2

When a section has to be played twice, a pair of dots is placed at the beginning of the section and another at the end. Used in this way the dots act as buffers, bouncing you back to the previous set of dots. When there is only one set, the repeat is made back to the beginning of the piece.

A slur is a curved line placed over or under notes of a different pitch. It indicates that the notes contained within the slur are to be played as smoothly as possible.

GERMAN DANCE

Allegretto — **L. van Beethoven**

mp ... *mf*

Tone development

When slurs occur over notes played in the same slide position (or notes that use the same valve combination), the notes are played smoothly in one continuous breath. Only the first note is tongued. To help develop this technique, practise the next set of exercises carrying out the following drill.

1. Produce the upward slur by a small contraction of the embouchure muscles: at the same time slightly raise the tongue and diaphragm levels.
2. In bar 2, breathe through the corners of the mouth keeping the embouchure formation as still as possible.
3. Produce the downward slur by a small relaxation of the embouchure muscles and a slight lowering of the tongue and diaphragm levels.
4. Repeat exercise (a) using the notes shown in exercises (b) (c) and (d). Euphonium players should use valves 1 and 3 (or 4) for both notes in exercise (d).

DUO

Adapted from "St. Petersburg"

Andante — **Dmitry Bortniansky**

CONCERT PIECES FOR UNITS 1-8

Piano accompaniments to the concert pieces are available in a separate accompaniment book. These should be used to provide experience in playing with an accompanist. 'Chorus' by Gluck is an example of music that has been set for early grade examinations.

SERENADE

from "Twelve Short Pieces" op. 125

ANTONIO DIABELLI
(1781 - 1856)
arr. PETER WASTALL

CHORUS

from "Paris and Helen"

C. W. GLUCK
(1714 - 1787)
arr. PETER WASTALL

AUTUMN GOLD

ANDANTE

from "First steps" op. 82

CORNELIUS GURLITT
(1820 - 1901)
arr. PETER WASTALL

UNIT 9

A New Note

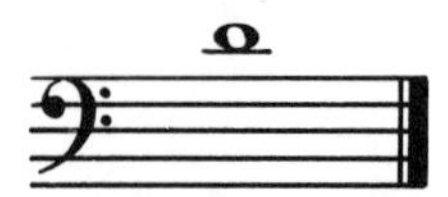

1

Euphonium fingering

open

Accidentals

*Because of the accidental, both these notes are A♭.

When a flat (or sharp) is used that is not in the key-signature it is called an accidental. An accidental lasts until the next bar-line and because of this, affects any subsequent note of the same pitch in that bar.

Tone development

1. Use the first note to establish a good embouchure formation.
2. In bars 2 and 3, check that the tongue and diaphragm levels move slightly up when the notes ascend, and move slightly down when the notes descend.
3. Pay strict attention to the slurs; even if a note fails to "speak", resist the temptation to tongue it.
4. Repeat exercise (a) using the notes shown in exercises (b) (c) (d) and (e).

UNIT 10

Accent Signs

An accent sign placed over or under a note means that the note must be given a strong attack with the tongue. Often this strong attack is combined with a little 'punch' from the diaphragm.

Dotted Crotchets

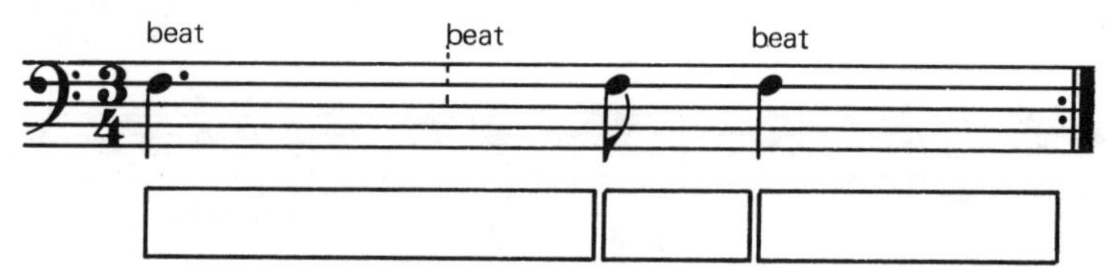

Since a dot after a note lengthens that note by half its value, the value of a dotted crotchet will be one and a half crotchet beats, the same length of sound as three quavers added together. Look at the example, then study the similarity of bars 2 and 3 in the first exercise.

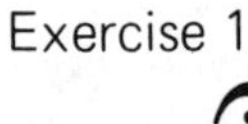

Exercise 1

Exercise 2

Exercise 3

THE EMPEROR OF GERMANY'S MARCH

Tone development

1. Ensure maximum flexibility by using a minimum amount of mouthpiece pressure against the lips.
2. Listen carefully to the sound and do not tolerate a pinched, nasal tone quality.
3. Breathe through the corners of the mouth, keeping the embouchure formation as still as possible.
4. Use the rhythm of the exercise to help develop embouchure control.
5. Repeat exercise (a) using the notes shown in exercises (b) (c) (d) and (e).

UNIT 11

New Notes

B

4

F♯

5

Euphonium fingering

1
2

2
3

Sharp Signs

The sign for raising a note by half a tone is called a sharp. Like the flat sign, it can be placed immediately before the note it affects or it can be placed at the beginning of each staff to form a key-signature.

A New Key-signature

The two keys that have no flats or sharps in their key-signature are: C Major and A Minor. 'Cradle Song' by Brahms is an example of music in C Major.

CRADLE SONG

Tone development

1. Concentrate on a muscular contraction of the embouchure for playing these smaller interval lip slurs.
2. Use bars 1 and 2 to establish the muscular feel of the exercise.
3. Play bar 3 at a speed comfortable to your embouchure development.
4. Repeat exercise (a) using the notes shown in exercises (b), (c), (d) and (e).

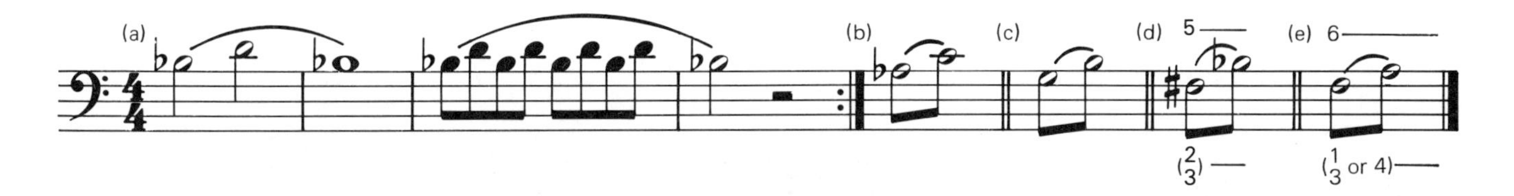

LITTLE ELEGY

UNIT 12

Natural Signs

A natural sign is used to cancel a flat or sharp. Since it is a type of accidental, it will only last for the bar in which it is printed. However, if a note that has been altered occurs again in the next bar, an additional accidental is often used to confirm that the note has returned to its original pitch.

Italian terms

pp	very soft	*ff*	very loud
p	soft	*f*	loud
mp	moderately soft	*mf*	moderately loud
> (diminuendo hairpin)	gradually softer	< (crescendo hairpin)	gradually louder

Italian terms also describe the mood of a piece, changes of speed and large repeats such as da capo. As with Italian terms introduced earlier, English translations can be found at the end of the book.

A table of Italian terms which show how loud or soft the music should sound is printed above. It should be used in conjunction with the tuning technique introduced in this unit.

Exercise 1

Exercise 2

Exercise 3

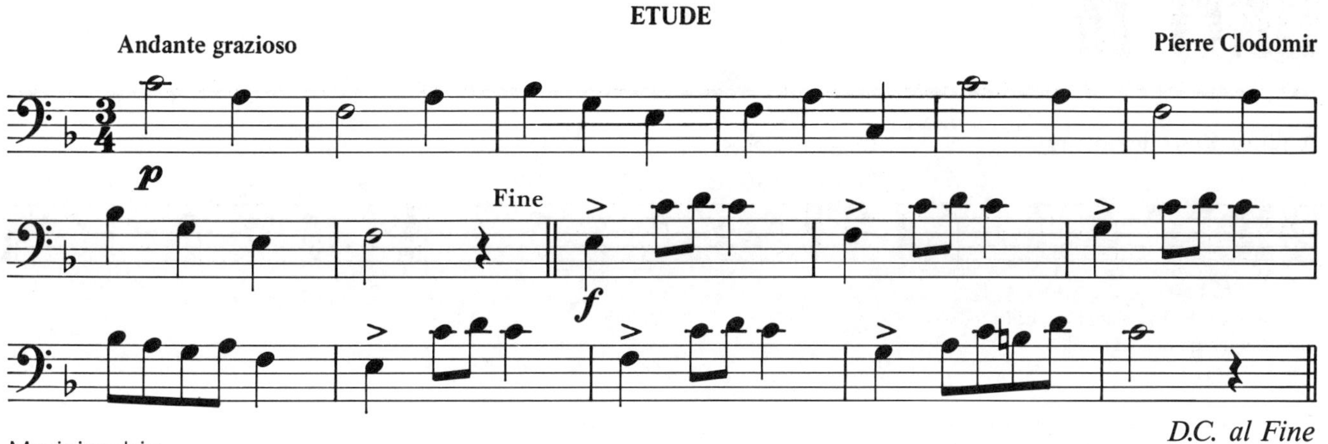

Musicianship

Crescendos and diminuendos play an important part in creating expression but need careful use since they also have an effect on tuning. Basically, a crescendo (produced by increasing the air pressure) will make a note go sharp, and a diminuendo (produced by reducing the air pressure) will make a note go flat.

To stabilise the tuning, allow the lip aperture to open slightly during a crescendo, and close slightly during a diminuendo.

UNIT 13

A New Key-signature

*Because of the key-signature, both these notes must be played as F♯.

The two keys that use the key-signature with one sharp are: G Major and E Minor. 'Lullaby' by Schubert is an example of music in G Major.

Quaver Rests

A quaver rest is a rest for half a crotchet beat. Bar 1 of the example shows it occurring on the second half of a crotchet beat, and bar 2 on the first half. The rhythmic difference between the two rhythms should be clearly understood before playing their related exercises.

Minor Keys

To find the name of a minor key, count three letter names down inclusive from the name of the major key. To find out whether the music is in a major key or a minor key, compare it with the appropriate scale.

Exercise 1

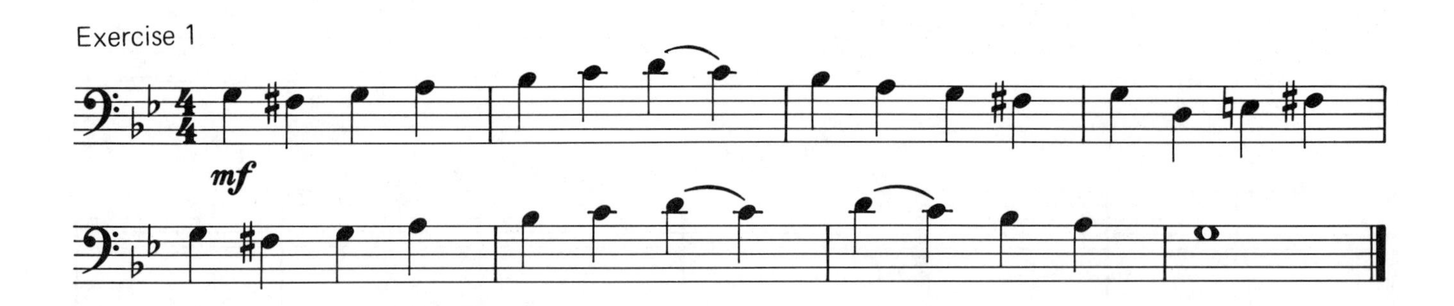

Exercise 2

Exercise 3

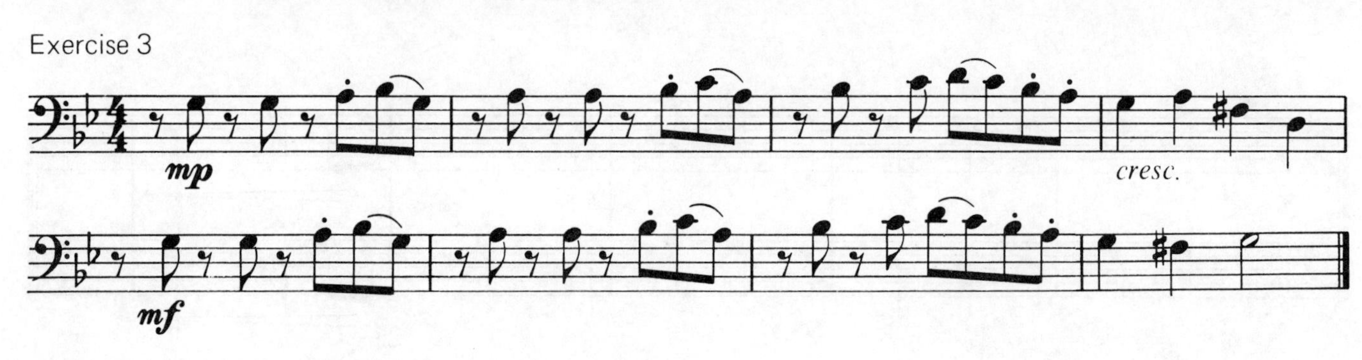

Scales and arpeggios:

G Minor (harmonic form) to be played from memory

Trombone technique

1. Start with the best possible tone, then spread it to the note below.
2. Produce the descending slurs by carefully co-ordinating the embouchure changes with the changes of slide position.
3. Eliminate unwanted sounds by using a fast, precise slide movement.
4. Play D in fourth position and B♭ in fifth position where indicated.

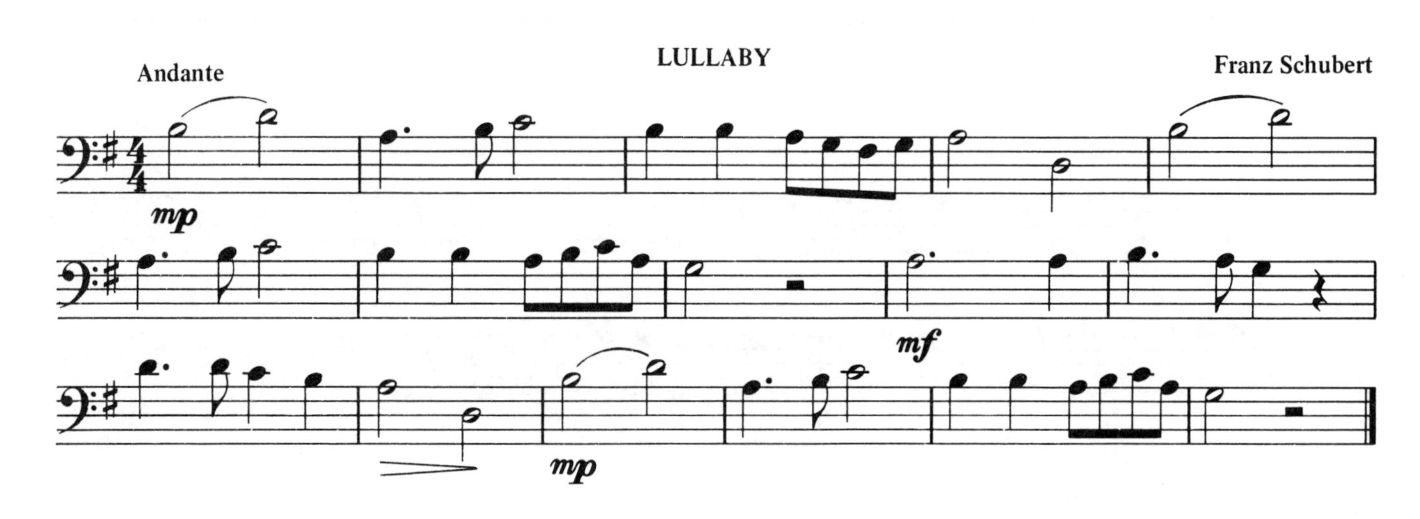

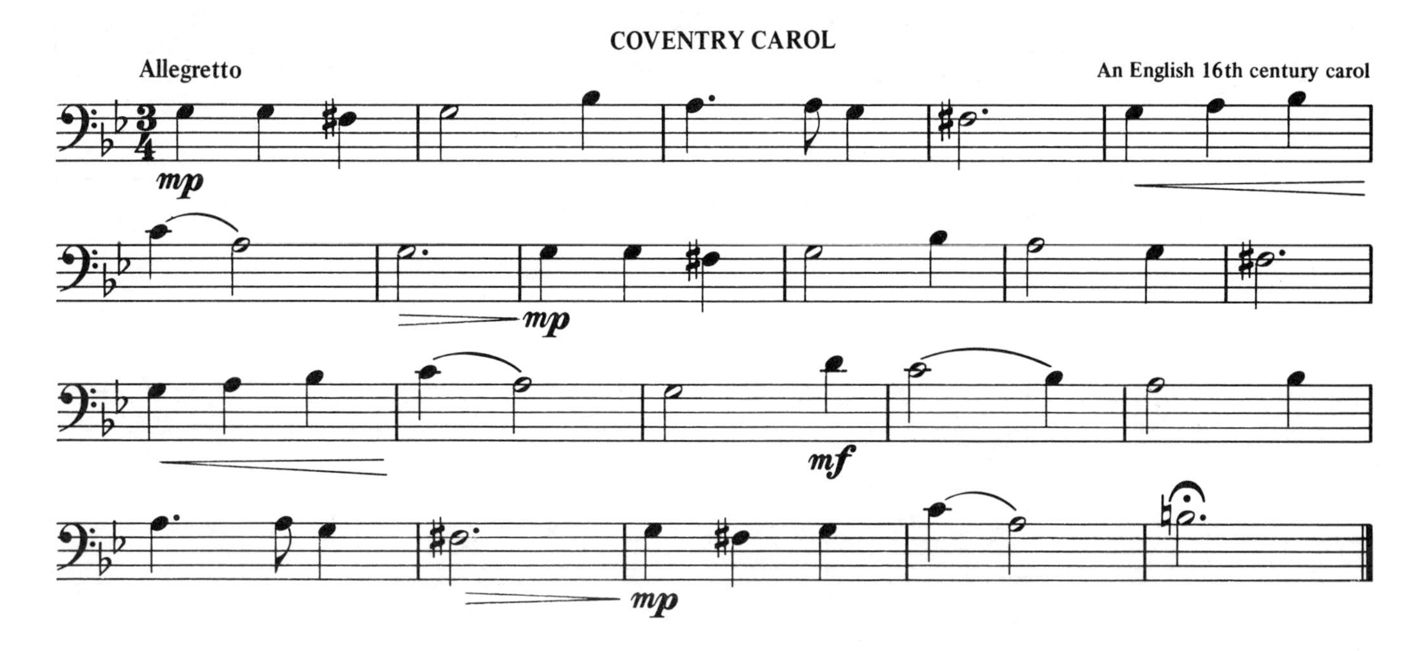

UNIT 14

Compound Time

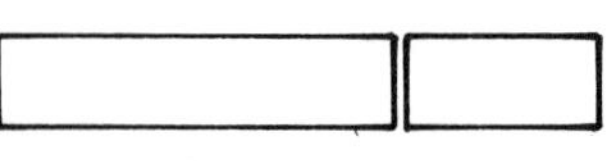

= one whole beat

When the natural pulse of a piece divides itself into thirds of a beat, the music is said to be in compound time. The various notes retain the same value in relation to each other; for instance there are still two quavers in a crotchet, but their value in relation to the beat is changed to the values shown in the example.

Compound Time-signatures

To show the new note values a new set of time-signatures is used. The example shows six-eight, indicating two dotted crotchet beats in a bar. A chart showing the complete range of compound time-signatures and how they are applied is printed at the end of the book.

Exercise 1

Exercise 2

Exercise 3

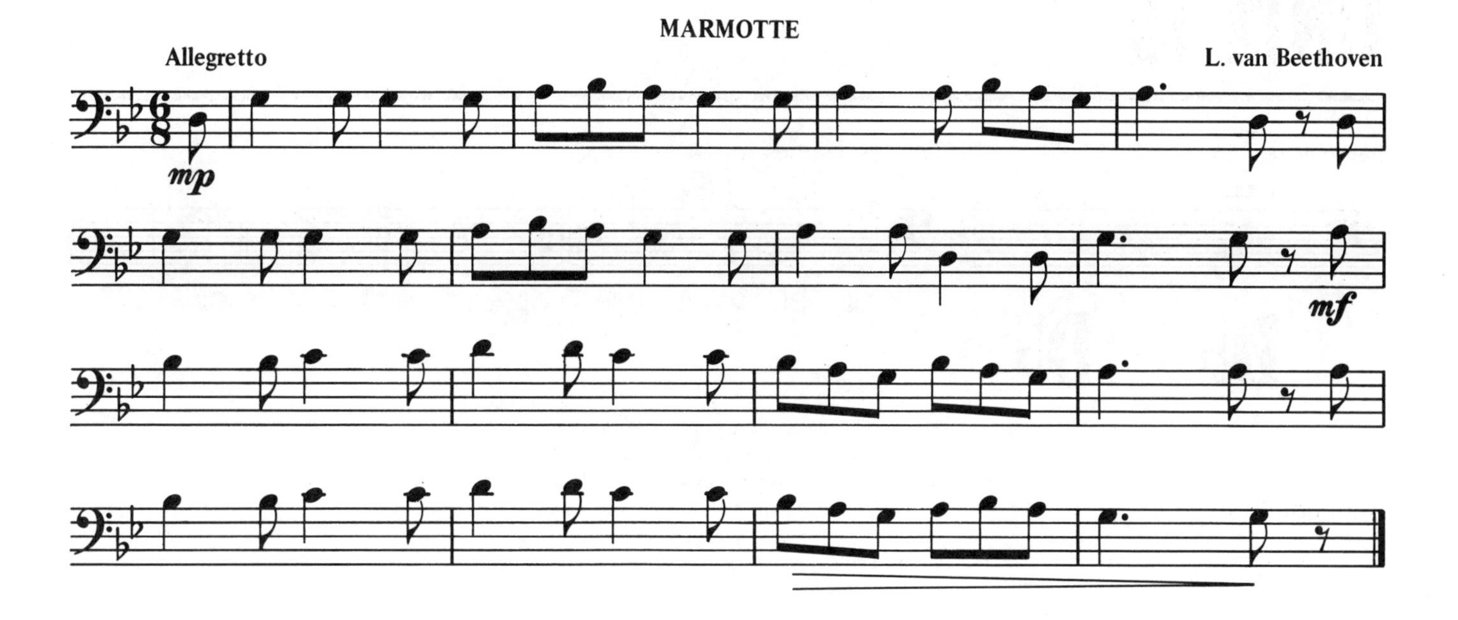

Aids to music reading

When reading notes which are thirds of a beat, read them as if they were three-syllable words. As an example of this, try the first exercise thinking the word TENTATIVE as you play each group. When playing the pieces, apply this reading principle to all rhythmic groups contained within one beat.

UNIT 15

New Notes

D♭ **D♭**

2 5

Euphonium fingering

2 2
3

Double Names for Notes

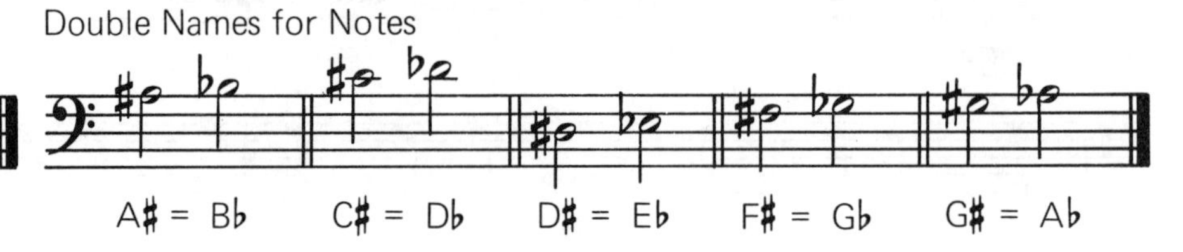

The interval between A and B is one whole tone. Since a sharp raises a note by half a tone, and a flat lowers a note by half a tone, it follows that A♯ and B♭ are different names for the name note. Double names can be given to all the flats and sharps learned so far.

Exercise 1

Exercise 2

Exercise 3

Scales and arpeggios

D Minor (harmonic form) to be played from memory

Tone development

1. Start with a small accent, then carefully follow the dynamics.
2. Produce the second note by choosing just the right amount of controlled physical relaxation.
3. Remember that rests between the exercises are almost as important as the exercises themselves.
4. Repeat exercise (a) using the notes shown in exercises (b) (c) (d) (e) and (f).

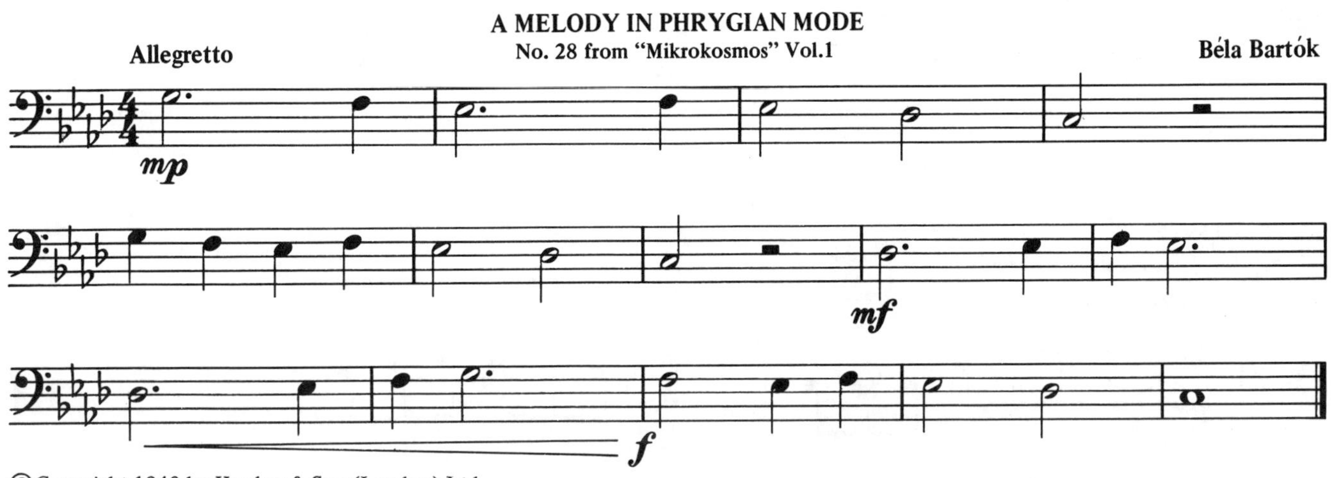

UNIT 16

Tenuto Signs

1st and 2nd time bars

A tenuto sign placed over or under a note means that the note is to be played with a lingering pressure. Usually it is also associated with a type of tonguing where one syllable is added to another without any noticeable break in the air stream.

Sometimes the ending of a repeated section is altered the second time through. When this occurs, 1st and 2nd time bars are used. The example is taken from "Ein' feste Burg", in which bars 1 - 4 are played quite normally the first time through, but when they are repeated the first time bar is omitted and the second time bar played instead.

Musicianship

Sometimes the general character of a piece suggests that many of the notes should be played staccato. When this occurs, the dots on top of the notes are often omitted, leaving it to the instrumentalist to interpret the music in a staccato style. The "Fanfare" by André Campra is an example of this.

CONCERT PIECES FOR UNITS 9 - 16

As with earlier concert pieces, piano accompaniments should be used to provide experience in playing with an accompanist. 'The Sandman' by Brahms is an example of music that has been set for early grade examinations.

THE SANDMAN

MIDNIGHT IN TOBAGO

THE HANDBONE MAN

KEITH RAMON COLE

* Omit gliss. when played on Euphonium.

UNIT 17

A New Note

3

Euphonium fingering

1

Grace Notes

In their simplest form, grace notes are notes added to a melody to make the music sound more decorative. To show how they are used, first play the example without the pair of grace notes, then again, using the grace notes to decorate the second A. As a general rule, grace notes should be played gracefully and lightly.

STUDY No.1

from 'Method for the Ophiclide'

ON WINGS OF SONG

Tone development

1. Use these exercises to continue the development of tongue and diaphragm co-ordination.
2. For downward slurs (notes 2 and 4), form an 'AAA' syllable and enlarge the mouth cavity by slightly opening the gap between the teeth.
3. For upward slurs (notes 3 and 5) help the embouchure contraction by forming either an 'OOO' syllable or an 'EEE' syllable, depending on the pitch of the note.
4. As before, repeat exercise (a) using the positions and fingerings indicated.

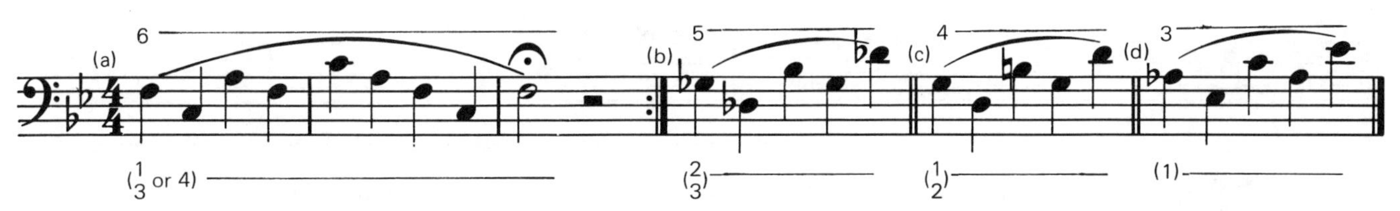

MARCH

UNIT 18

Semiquavers

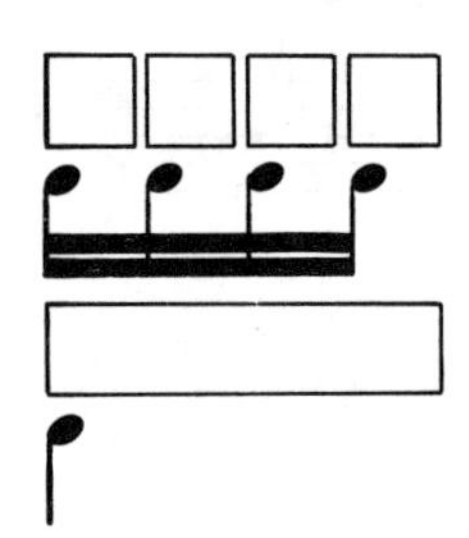

The value of a semiquaver is a quarter of a crotchet; it is printed with two tails on the end of its stem. As with quavers all the tails contained in one beat can be joined together.

Syncopation

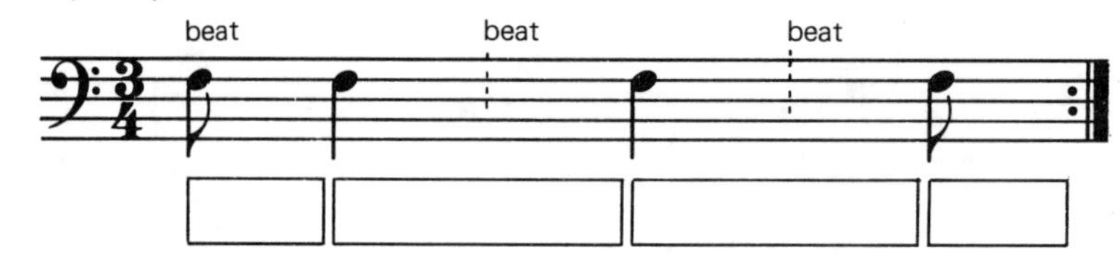

A new rhythm, called syncopation, is produced when strongly accented notes occur between the beats instead of coinciding with them.

As shown in the duet, the surrounding quavers are usually played staccato to help bounce the syncopated notes off the beat.

Exercise 1

Exercise 2

Scales and arpeggios

E♭ Major, to be played from memory.

LARGHETTO

Aids to music reading

With blocks of four semiquavers, read each group as you would a four-syllable word. Start with passages that are easy to play (such as the two exercises shown opposite) and make a conscious effort to read each block of four semiquavers as a single unit.

A SYNCOPATED DUET

UNIT 19

A New Note

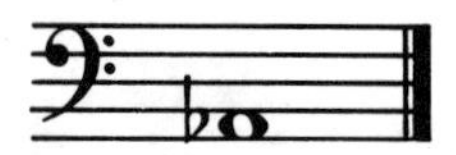

3

Euphonium fingering

1

Dotted Quavers

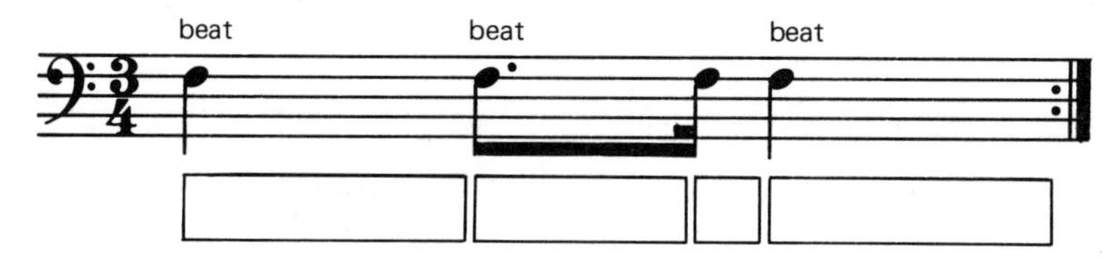

A dotted quaver, or its equivalent rest, lasts for three quarters of a crotchet-beat. Usually it is combined with a single semiquaver since this completes the beat.

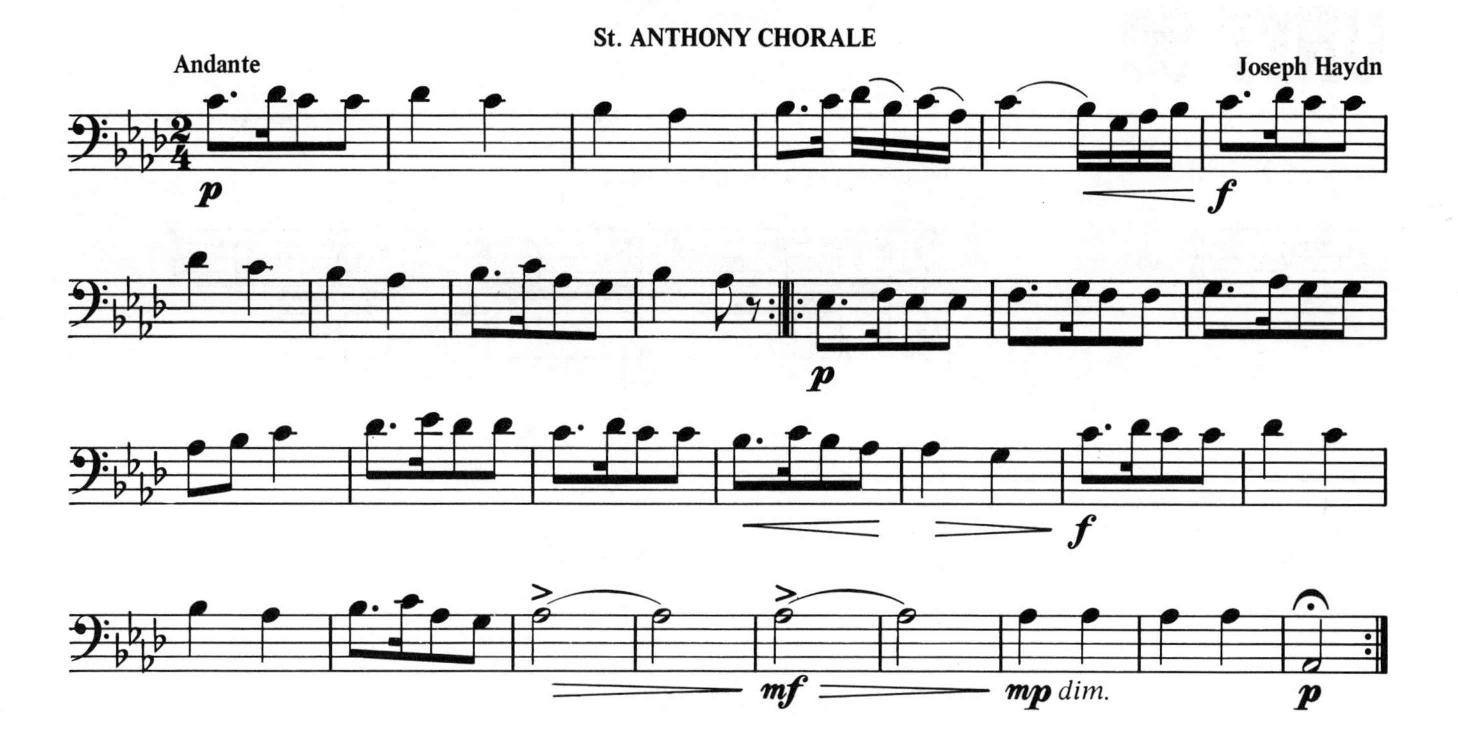

Aids to music reading

The reading technique for a single semiquaver is to group the semiquaver with the note which follows. In lively movements, a useful way to achieve this is to pronounce the two notes as if saying the word TODAY. As an example, play the first note of the "Soldier's March" by Schumann, then think TODAY as you play the next two notes. This reading technique can be used every time a dotted rhythm occurs.

UNIT 20

Semiquaver Rests

A semiquaver rest is a rest for a quarter of a crotchet beat. Notice that it is similar to the semiquaver note, being printed with two tails. An example of the semiquaver rest can be found in the duet.

Note patterns using Semiquavers

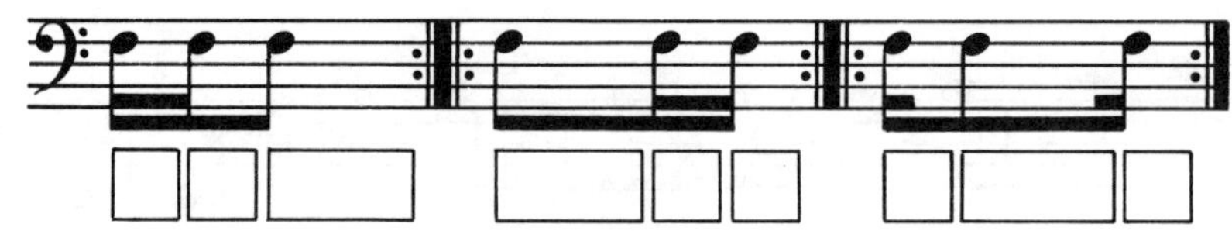

By combining semiquavers with quavers, several new rhythm patterns can be formed. The above examples should be studied carefully before playing the exercises.

Tone development

1. Descend by relaxation, making sure the facial muscles remain under control.
2. If the lower notes fail to respond, check the pressure of the mouthpiece against the lips; remember, for lower tones the bottom lip in particular must be free to vibrate.
3. If a note fails to 'speak' in the ascending slur, resist the temptation to tongue it; instead, take a small rest then try the exercise one semitone lower.
4. Repeat exercise (a) using the notes shown in exercises (b) (c) and (d).

UNIT 21

A New Note

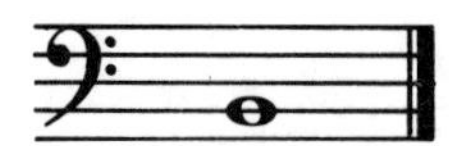

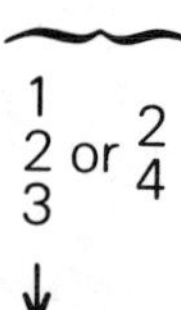

Euphonium fingering

1
2 or 2
3   4

Three-eight Time

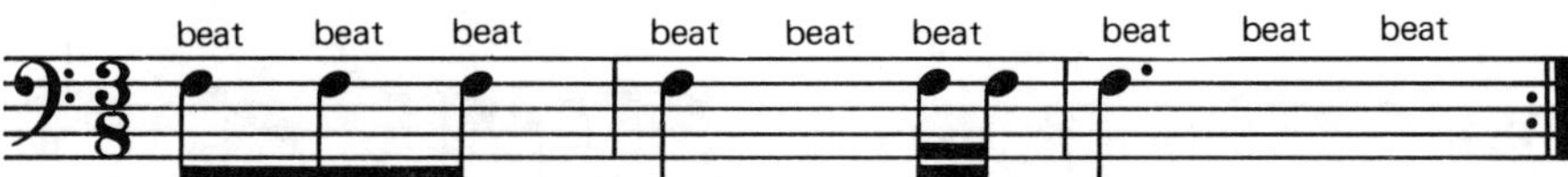

The time-signature of three-eight indicates that there are three quaver beats in each bar. As before, the various notes retain the same value in relation to each other. It is the value of the notes in relation to the beat that is changed.

* Fingering 1-2-3 is very sharp in pitch. Lip down to the correct tuning.

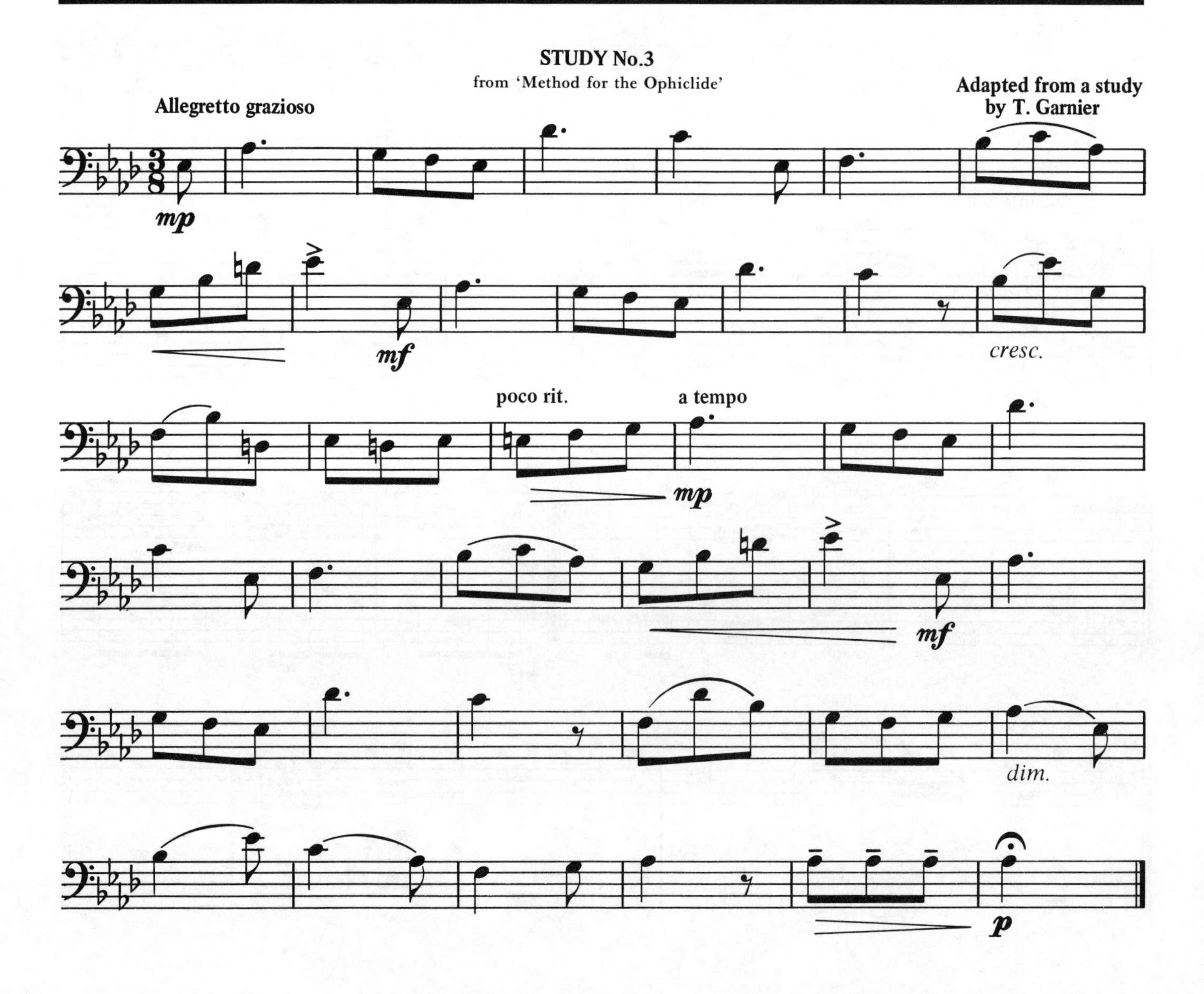

A LITTLE PIECE

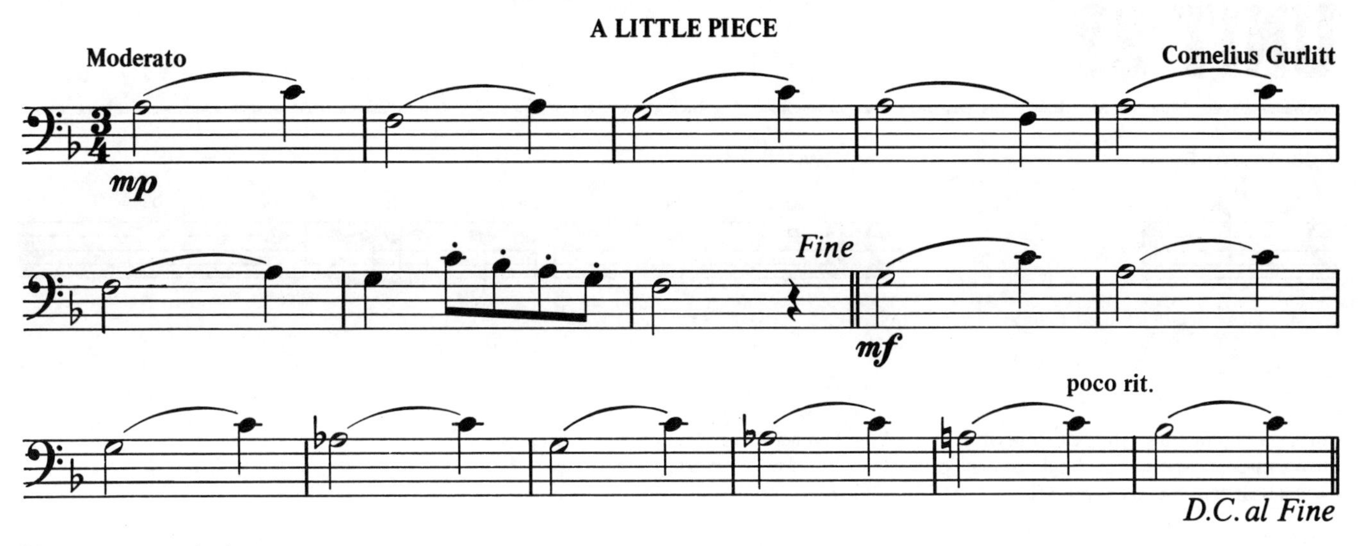

Trombone technique

1. Start with the best possible tone.
2. Having achieved a good tone, spread it to the note above. (Check the tuning of the upper note).
3. As in unit 13, eliminate unwanted sounds by using a fast, precise slide movement.
4. Remember that ascending slurs need careful control of the air pressure if a smooth embouchure change is to be achieved.

LAND OF OUR FATHERS

UNIT 22

Acciaccaturas

An acciaccatura is a small grace note with a stroke through its stem. It should be played on the beat and as short as possible.

Two-two Time

The time signature of two two indicates that there are two minim beats in each bar. The value of the notes in relation to the beat is shown in the example. Sometimes two-two is called Alla Breve.

Exercise 1

Scales and arpeggios

C Minor (harmonic form) to be played from memory.

Trombone scale passages and arpeggios

C Minor (harmonic form) to be played from memory.

A Major arpeggio, to be played from memory.

B♭ Major arpeggio, to be played from memory.

ANDANTE

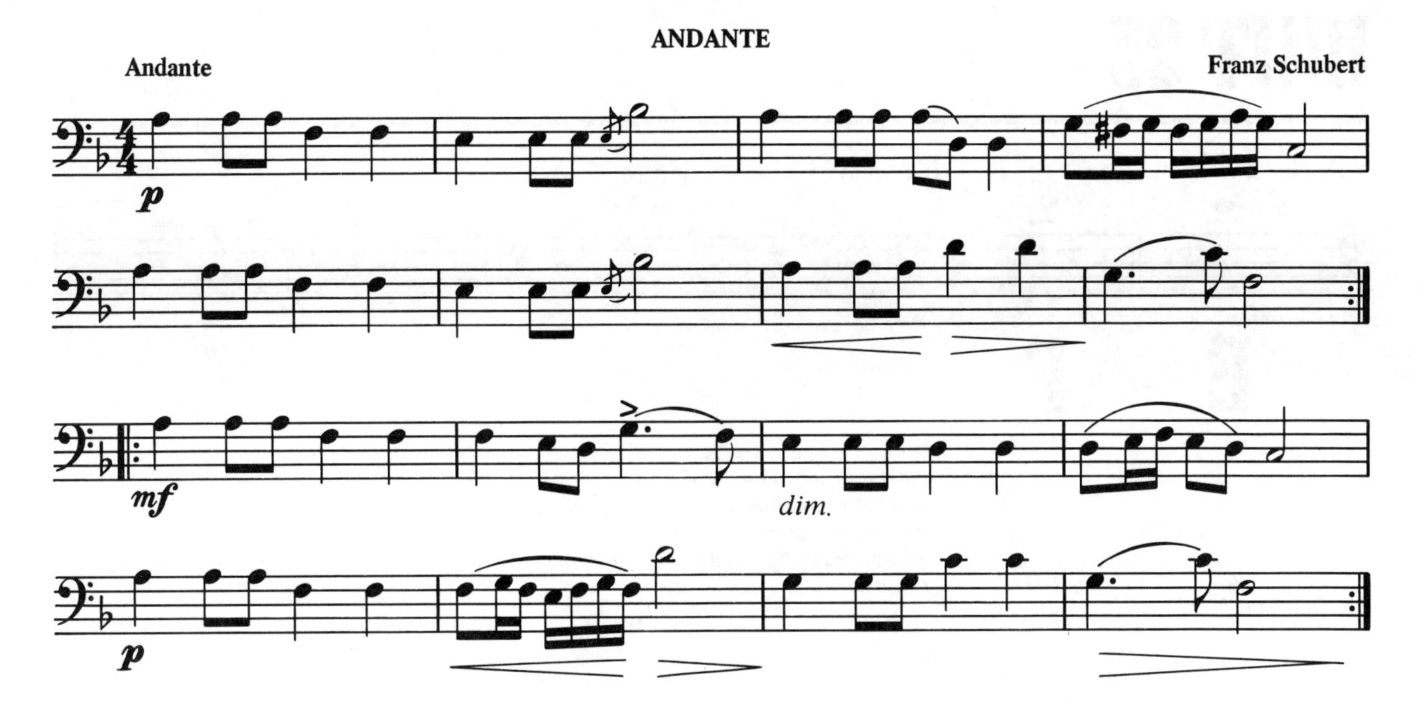

Trombone technique

When slurs are placed over a whole series of notes (Schubert 'Andante', bars 4, 12 and 14) they indicate that the phrase is to be played in a legato style. Glissandos must be avoided so a very gentle type of tonguing is used, rather like pronouncing the syllable DAH. The actual syllable varies considerably from player to player, and even from phrase to phrase. The important thing is to perform the phrase smoothly with the smallest perceptible interruption between the notes.

COTILLON

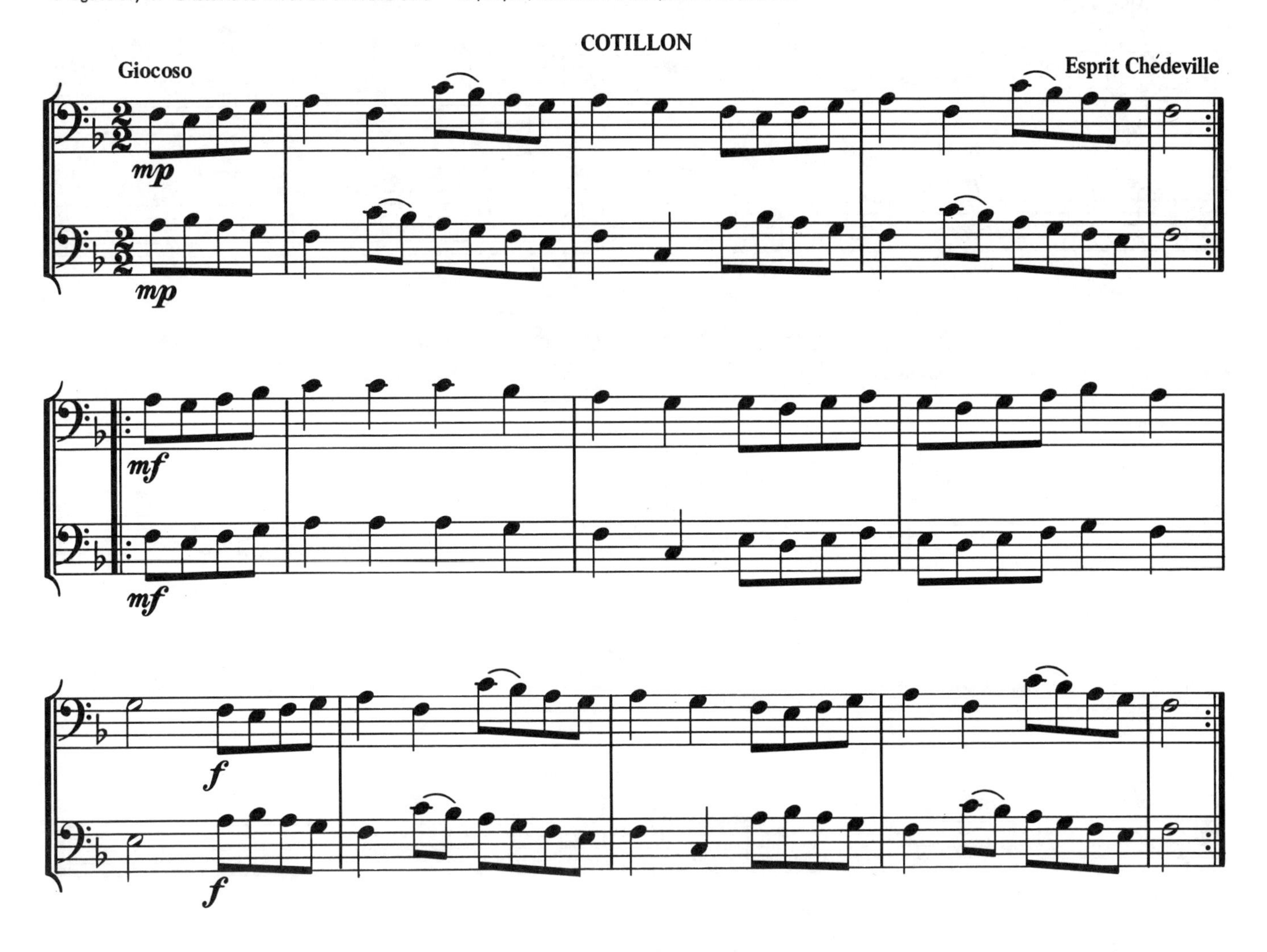

UNIT 23

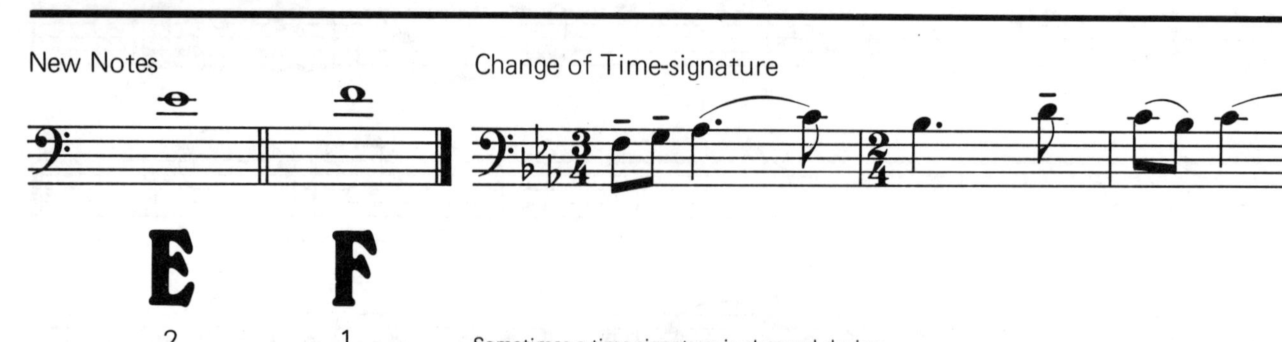

Euphonium fingering

2 open

Sometimes a time-signature is changed during the course of a piece. When this occurs the speed of the beat usually remains the same; it is the pulse pattern that changes. The example is taken from the "Cantilena" by Árpád Balázs.

Tone development

1. Use the first note to check and establish the embouchure formation.
2. Start the lip-slur with a 'TOOO' syllable, then use relaxation and a slightly lower tongue-level to produce the second note.
3. For notes 3 and 5, raise the tongue-level, making sure the diaphragm is giving co-ordinated support.
4. Repeat exercise (a) in each slide position (valve combination), starting on the notes shown.

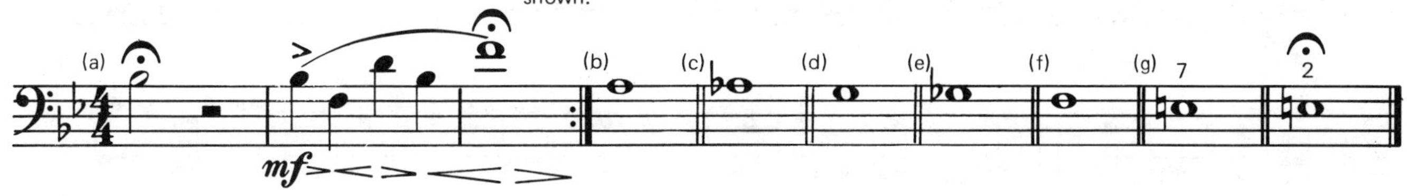

UNIT 24

Triplets

Rests of Several Bars

A New Key-signature

A triplet can be defined as 'three notes played in the time of two notes of the same value' (for instance, three quavers played in the time of two quavers). The number 3 is placed over or under them to show the momentary change of note value.

When a rest of several bars is required, only one bar is used; a black line is usually drawn in this bar, and the number of complete bars to be counted placed on top. The example is taken from the concert piece on p.60.

In sharp key, the name of the major key can be found by counting one letter name up from the last sharp. The scale of D Major has a key-signature with two sharps. Since the last sharp is C♯, the name of the key must be D Major.

Exercise 1

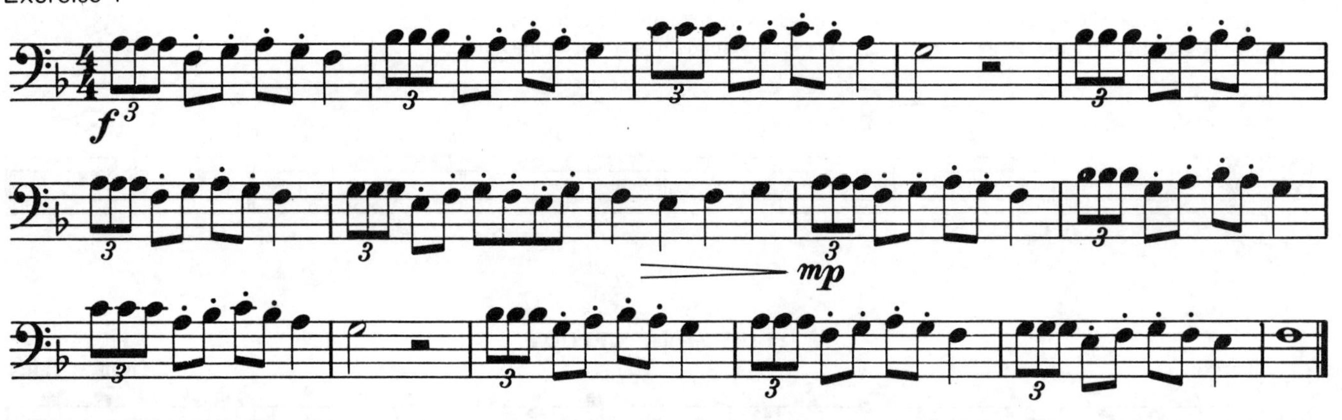

Scales and arpeggios:

Musicianship

Both pieces in this unit have performing directions relating to their mood: the Handel "Aria" is marked dolce espressivo, and the Mozart "Minuet" grazioso. As you practise, try to create these moods, and in particular use the shapes of the phrases for displaying control over the dynamics. In the "Aria", the repeated notes create good opportunities for expressive tenuto playing; the important thing to remember is that performing directions are a starting point for creating your own expression.

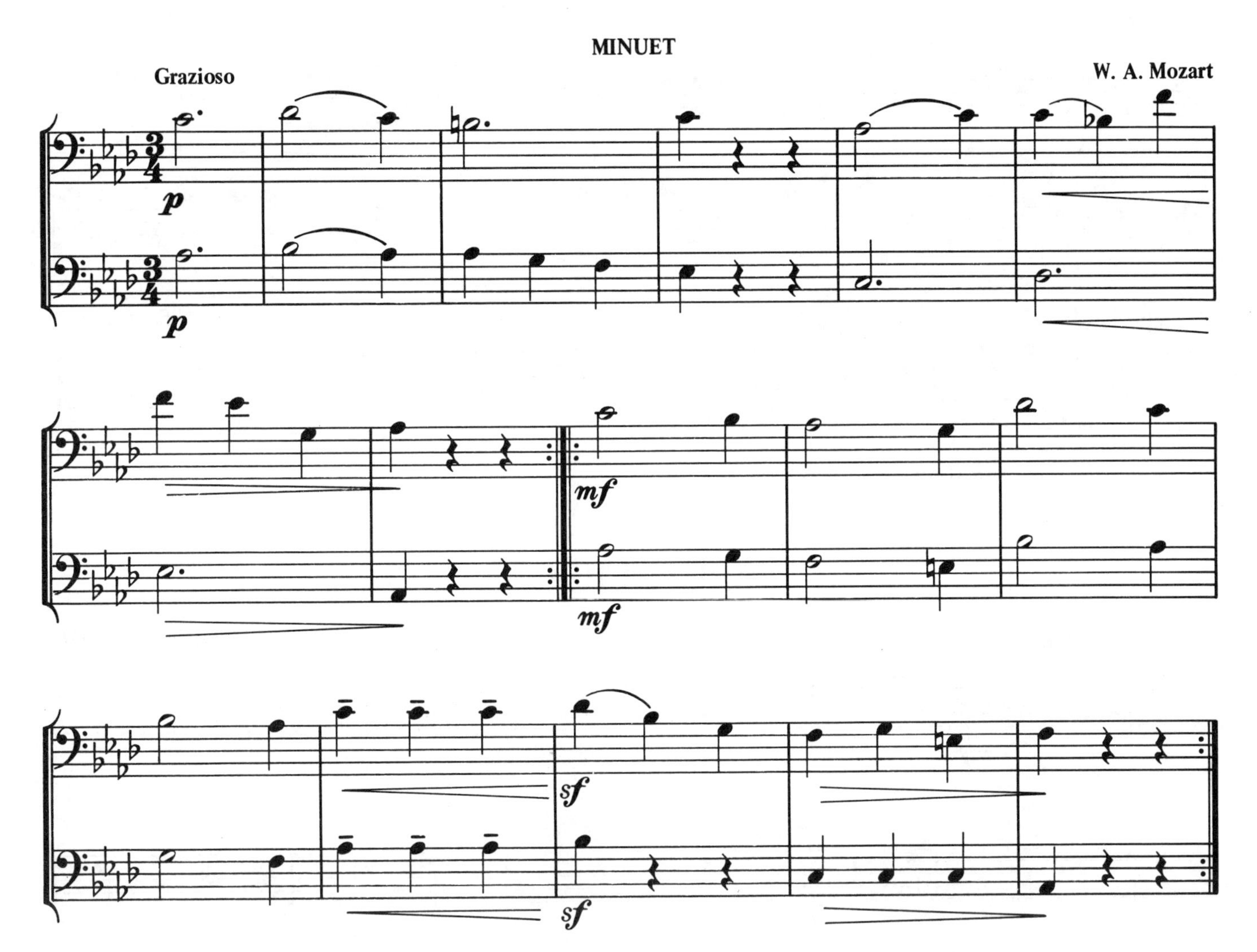

CONCERT PIECES FOR UNITS 17-24

'Pavan' by Byrd is an example of music that has been set for early grade examinations.

OXFORD BLUES

SOLILOQUY

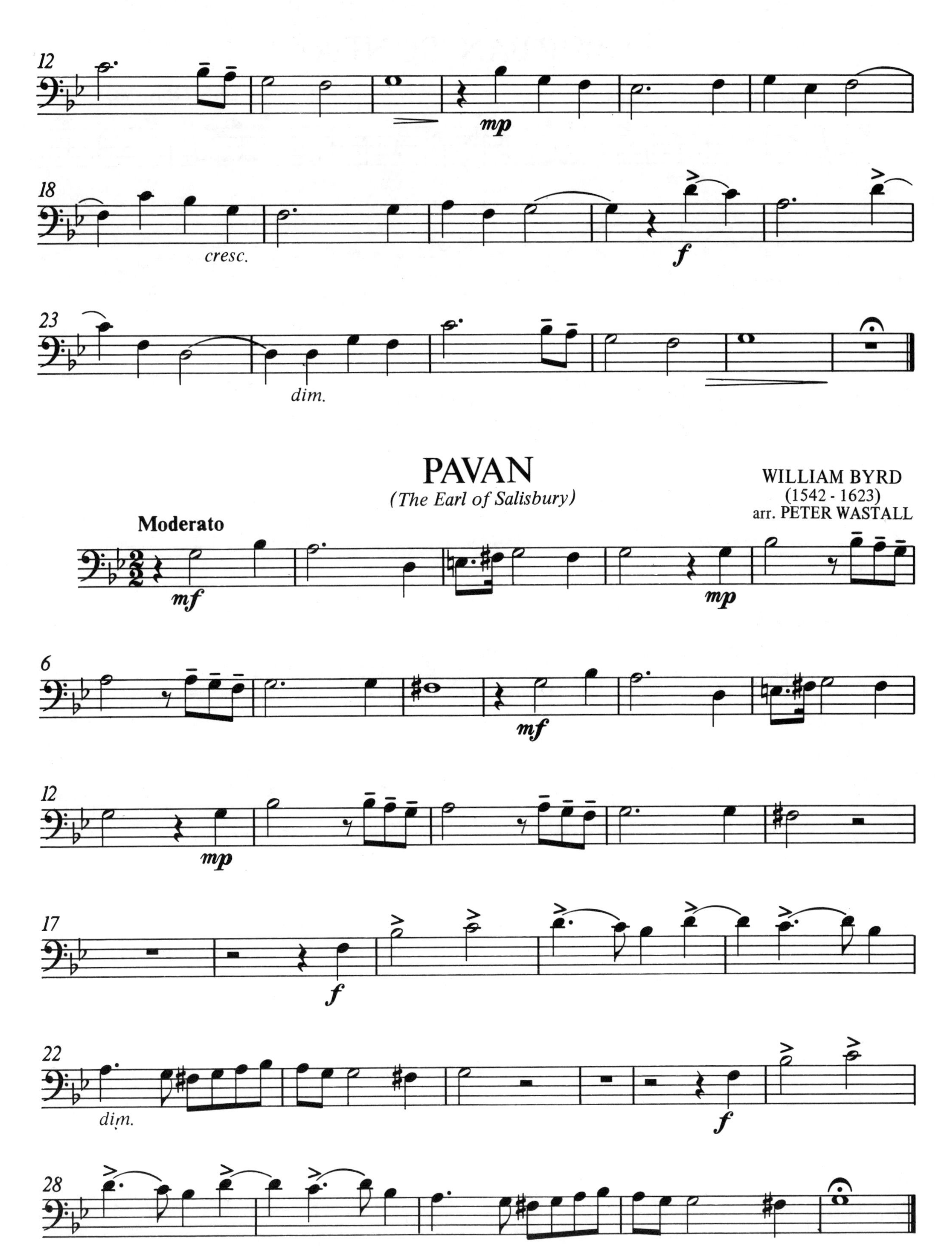
12
mp
18
cresc.
f
23
dim.
PAVAN
(The Earl of Salisbury)
WILLIAM BYRD
(1542 - 1623)
arr. PETER WASTALL
Moderato
mf
mp
6
mf
12
mp
17
f
22
dim.
f
28

SUBURBAN SUNDAY

KEITH RAMON COLE

45
mp
50
3
3
AIR
from "Richard Coeur de Lion"
ANDRE GRETRY
(1741 - 1813)
arr. PETER WASTALL
Moderato
mp
6
p
12
mf
18
mf
24
mp
30
p
36

SLIDE POSITION CHART

D♭ D E♭ E F F♯ G A♭ A B♭

2 1 3 2 1 3-* 2- 3 2 1

* Minus sign = shortened position

FINGERING CHART

E	F	F♯	G	A♭	A	B♭	B	C	D♭	D
1* 2 or 2 3 4 ↓	1 or 4 3	2 3	1 2	1	2	Open	1* 2 or 2 3 4 ↓	1 or 4 3	2 3	1 2

E♭	E	F	F♯	G	A♭	A	B♭	B	C
1	2	Open	2 3	1 2	1	2	Open	1 2	1

* Fingering 1-2-3 is very sharp in pitch. On instruments without a fourth valve lip down to correct the tuning.

TIME SIGNATURES

1. Look up the time signature

2. Look in the left hand column to find the number of beats in each bar.

3. Look in the top row above the time signature to find the type of note that equals one beat.

	Simple time			Compound time		
Value of each beat (type of note)	𝅗𝅥	♩	♪	𝅗𝅥.	♩.	♪.
Value of each beat as a fraction of a semibreve	$\frac{1}{2}$	$\frac{1}{4}$	$\frac{1}{8}$	$\frac{3}{4}$	$\frac{3}{8}$	$\frac{3}{16}$
2 beats in each bar	2/2	2/4	2/8	6/4	6/8	6/16
3 beats in each bar	3/2	3/4	3/8	9/4	9/8	9/16
4 beats in each bar	4/2	4/4	4/8	12/4	12/8	12/16

ITALIAN TERMS

A tempo Resume the normal speed.
Accelerando Becoming gradually faster.
Adagio Slow, leisurely.
Agitato Agitated.
Alla marcia In the style of a march.
Allargando Broadening out.
Allegretto Slightly slower than Allegro.
Allegro Lively, reasonably fast.
Andante (lit. walking) At a moderate pace.
Andantino A little andante.
Animato Animated.
Cantabile In a singing style.
Con With.
Crescendo *(cresc.)* Becoming louder.
Da Capo (D.C.) al Fine Back to the beginning and finish at the word Fine.
Dal Segno (D. S.) From the sign 𝄋
Deciso Decisively, firmly.
Diminuendo *(dim.)* Becoming gradually softer.
Dolce Sweetly.
E, Ed And.
Espressivo *(espress.)* With expression, with feeling.
Forte (*f*) Loud.
Fortissimo (*ff*) Very loud.
Giocoso Humorously.
Grazioso Gracefully.
Largo Slow and stately, broad.
Larghetto Less slow than Largo.
Legato Smoothly.
Leggiero Lightly.
Lento Slowly.
Maestoso Majestically.
Meno mosso Less movement.
Mezzo forte (*mf*) Moderately loud.
Mezzo piano (*mp*) Moderately soft.
Moderato Moderate time.
Molto Much.
Moto Movement.
Non troppo Not too much.
Pianissimo (*pp*) Very soft.
Piano (*p*) Soft.
Più mosso More movement, quicker.
Poco a poco Little by little (gradually).
Pomposo Pompously.
Presto Very quick.
Quasi As if, almost.
Rallentando (rall.) Becoming gradually slower.
Ritenuto (rit.) Hold back (slower at once).
Rubato Flexibly.
Semplice Simple.
Sempre Always.
Sforzando (*sf*, *sfz*) Forcing, accented.
Solenne Solemn.
Sonore Sonorous, full toned.
Sostenuto Sustained.
Spirito Spirit, life, energy.
Tempo I Resume the original speed.
Tenuto Held.
Tranquillo Quietly.
Un poco A little.
Vivace Lively, quick.